D1367136

Chats on Old Glass

FRONTISPIECE

An extremely rare Elizabethan goblet made by Verzelini and engraved in diamond-point by Anthony de Lysle. The initials A.T. and R.T. suggest that it was made to commemorate a wedding. Height $8\frac{3}{8}$ inches. Thus far, only nine vessels by Verzelini are known. They include a tazza-shaped goblet in the Musée de Cluny, dated 1578, the "John and Jone Dier" glass in the Victoria and Albert Museum, dated 1581, two goblets in The Corning Museum of Glass, dated 1577 and 1583, the earliest known dated English drinking vessel, and the gilded "Geare" goblet.

[*Delomosne & Son, Ltd., London*]

Chats on Old Glass

BY

R. A. ROBERTSON

REVISED, WITH A NEW CHAPTER

ON AMERICAN GLASS BY

KENNETH M. WILSON

CURATOR, THE CORNING MUSEUM OF GLASS

Dover Publications, Inc., New York

Published in Canada by General Publishing Company, Ltd.,
30 Lesmill Road, Don Mills, Toronto, Ontario.
Published in the United Kingdom by Constable and Company, Ltd.,
10 Orange Street, London WC 2.

This Dover edition, first published in 1969,
is a revised and expanded republication of the work first published by
Ernest Benn Limited in 1954.

Standard Book Number: 486-22131-8
Library of Congress Catalog Card Number: 68-14051

Manufactured in the United States of America

DOVER PUBLICATIONS, INC.
180 Varick Street
New York, N.Y. 10014

PREFACE TO THE DOVER EDITION

IN revising *Chats on Old Glass* I have been conscious of a dual responsibility: to make additions and, where necessary, corrections in light of recently discovered knowledge, but at the same time to preserve the original character of the book as established by the author. The inclusion of additional illustrations of both representative and outstanding examples of glass from various periods should enhance the value of the book for everyone, and the additional chapter on American glass should appeal particularly to anyone especially interested in this subject. A selected bibliography of American glass and a brief list of museums in this country where glass of all types is exhibited have also been included.

KENNETH M. WILSON

Corning, New York
January, 1969

PREFACE TO THE FIRST EDITION

TO discuss *glass* in a discursive and entertaining way has been my object in writing this book. For that reason I hope its appeal may extend beyond the interest of collectors and aspiring collectors to a wider public, and that it will hold something of value for all who cherish the past and love beautiful things. Those who admire craftsmanship for its own sake and those who care for the details of decoration that give point and character to the furnishing of a home may find stimulation in these pages.

This is not a textbook, and I have been at no pains to present the subject with impersonal exactitude. On the contrary, my all too human prejudices suffer little, perhaps no, restraint. It may be that these prejudices find agreement in some as they will no doubt irritate others; yet if none is indifferent, I have no complaint.

The subject is fascinating in many ways, not least in that it links us to the Past, which appears, through the haze of time, to contain a life more leisured and spacious than is possible in this rackety and restless age. Of greater importance is the sense of Man's divinity, given us by the unbroken continuity of a craft whose roots reach down into antiquity. To the historian the study of glass gives the clue to forgotten social customs. Things too trivial to be recorded may yet have an important effect on the moods and feelings of men and so end by shaping the destiny of nations. An understanding of these seemingly inconsequential causes will explain subsequent actions and points of view. Jacobite glasses alone offer a rich field for research because of their intricate political symbolism.

These things apart, I hope the book is to be of practical use to aspiring collectors. No book, of course, is a substitute for practice, as a book can only convey imperfectly, if it conveys it at all, the knowledge derived from the senses of touch, sight and hearing when these have been developed by experience. What it may do is to widen the scope of practical knowledge and give that practical knowledge a deeper significance, by showing how craftsmen, at different periods in time, achieved their best results. In this way a comprehensive knowledge of the material and how it is made, and fashioned, and decorated, is essential to the equipment of every collector. I have tried to convey some part of this knowledge and have pointed the way to the sources of reliable information as well. Even so, this book can be nothing more than an introduction to what is a wide subject, but, I think, it can modestly claim to show what is, and what is not, good craftsmanship.

With a few exceptions, the illustrations I use are of pieces in museums that can be seen by the public. As far as possible I have tried to include illustrations of specimens from museums in all parts of the country. In this I acknowledge my indebtedness to Mr. Cyril Wallis, F.S.A., of the Royal Scottish Museum, Edinburgh.

Lastly, my inquiry into the subject turned out to be an exciting and exhilarating experience. If you have half the enjoyment in reading this book that I had in writing it, you have had your money's worth. What more do you want?

R. A. R.

Bathgate, Scotland

Contents

List of Illustrations

Plate *Following page*

Plate *Following page*

Chats on Old Glass

Chapter One

HOW GLASS IS MADE, FASHIONED, AND DECORATED

THE ENJOYMENT OF GLASS

THE notion of becoming a collector of glass may strike one out of the blue. Perhaps the elusive grace of some delicate piece seen in an antique shop or auction rooms catches the eye; perhaps, when taking tea with old Aunt Hester, one suddenly becomes aware of a wineglass among the accumulated rubbish and impedimenta with which that dear old soul clutters up her life, and then one cries out:

"Hello, what have we here?"

What, indeed! To old Aunt Hester the glass is a symbol of the social importance belonging to older and better days. Too volubly she is reminded of poor Papa (your great-grandfather, my dear) who kept a carriage and pair and three big dogs, or that awful Uncle Gerald who drove tandem and was once committed to an actress, although it would never have done.

Stanchlessly the flood of garrulity pours on. It becomes a mere twittering, a background of sound to one's thoughts. For the first time one sees the wineglass not as a sign of family magnificence, but of something having merit in its own right. Here in one's hand is a piece of art full of mystery and wonder. The substance is insubstantial, the form delicately wrought, and the whole has about it a quality seeming to go beyond the intention of the craftsman who made it, a hint of impressionism that reveals his character as surely as a signature reveals the character of a writer. It gives one a distinct pleasure to hold, it links one to the spirit of a past age and brings a rather warm aesthetic delight.

If that has happened to you, or if it is an experience that could happen to you, then you are a born collector. Now, although many have the desire to start making a collection, few do it. Considerations of cost stand in the way, and the timid or cautious draw back from making the first purchase that will lead to a fascinating pursuit lest they find themselves involved in a ruinous enterprise. Yet such fears are unfounded, for making a good collection is not beyond the man of moderate means who has a love of beauty in his soul and an eye for good craftsmanship.

But if one is actuated by mere acquisitiveness, by the desire to own something better than anyone else, the pursuit is not to be recommended. Taken in that spirit it will engender envy; and envy, we are told, is the root of unhappiness. Even a millionaire cannot buy everything, for there is always some other millionaire, luckier, wealthier, and even greedier than himself.

How different is the man who collects because he has a love of the subject. In his case the pursuit brings happiness, enlarges the mind, develops the faculties of appreciation and criticism, and makes him a more interesting person. Nor does the comparative poverty or insignificance of the collection diminish his pleasure. On the contrary, the collection having been made slowly, one piece at a time, is something that is his own, something that he alone could bring together, and from it he derives far more pleasure than a wealthier man who buys a case of glass at a time and never bothers to look at the individual pieces once he has it.

If a man starts collecting can he avoid mistakes? The answer is no, he can't. Even well-informed experts have been known to blunder, and with glass, as with everything else, experience has its price. Nevertheless, serious errors of judgment can be avoided, and the spurious is less likely to deceive if one has knowledge of the subject, if one is familiar with the history of glass and aware of the different achievements the many generations of glassworkers have contributed to the art throughout the ages. The purpose of this book is to give such information, but it does not pretend to be more than an introduction to what is a very wide subject. If it can influence some readers to make a closer study of the subject it will not have been written in vain, and, in the hope that it may do so, a list of the books likely to be helpful is included in this volume.

The cultivation of taste, however, demands contact with the best specimens of the art. Fortunately, the rarest pieces and the biggest collections are to be seen in our museums. These are everybody's collection, bought for your enjoyment. A list of the more important museums where glass is to be seen is also included in this book, and the student is advised to make frequent visits to the museum in his locality and to visit such as he conveniently can when he travels from home. But the recommendation is hardly necessary, for they who have discovered the wonder and mystery of glass will be drawn to these collections again and again, as a moth is drawn to the flame. Once the interest is kindled or the imagination touched, the pursuit becomes a passion and the hunt is up.

ORIGINS OF GLASS

Glass may be made by melting only silica, usually supplied in the form of sand from river beds and seashores, or ancient deposits left by them, but this requires such great heat that glass made in this way is not commercially practicable. If a flux, such as an alkali in the form of potash or soda ash, is added, the mixture will melt at the still high but easily attained temperature of 1300 degrees Centrigrade. Since such a fusion of silica and an alkali is soluble, it is necessary to add a third principal ingredient to form a readily made, stable glass. This is usually lime.

In its molten state the metal, as it is called by glassmakers, is sticky and tenacious. At red heat it is plastic and yielding, so that it is easily fashioned, and in that condition it is capable of being drawn into bars or even threads thinner than human hair. At red heat, too, it is easily welded. Two pieces of glass will join together and become inseparable with no more trouble than is involved in sticking two pieces of melted sealing wax together. But its most outstanding characteristic is that it can be blown in its plastic state like a bubble or balloon and thus easily shaped into hollow vessels.

While silica, lime, and a flux are the basic ingredients of glass (called, before it is fused, the batch), alumina, red lead, and other substances may be added to produce different qualities, such as durability or brilliancy, and in modern times boric oxide is used to make heat-resisting glass. Color is produced by adding to the batch small quantities of metallic oxides: copper, which produces blue, ruby, and some greens; cobalt, which gives a very dark blue; iron, which gives green; and so on through a list constantly being added to by modern chemistry.

The first glass to be made was colored, and certainly the Egyptians, who are, along with the Mesopotamians, at present, the earliest glassmakers known to us, were highly skilled in producing fine colors. Indeed, it is difficult to make glass entirely free of color. Little coloring matter is required to color the batch, so that if iron is present in the sand, even in minute quantities, completely colorless glass cannot be obtained. As it is hardly possible to find a sand quite free of iron, the effects of iron as a coloring agent have to be eradicated when the aim is to produce colorless glass. This can be done by adding decolorants, such as manganese, arsenic, antimony, cerium, or selenium, to the batch in very small quantities.

Today science has contributed much to the preparation of glass. Chemistry has made possible many types of glass adaptable to different purposes and has increased the range and variety of colors. Engineering has produced efficient furnaces in which heat is controlled with precision, which reduce fuel consumption, accelerate the process of melting, eliminate uncertainty, and make predictable results possible.

But it was not always so. In the seventeenth century, for example, when experiments were being made in England, Germany, and the Netherlands to find a suitable substitute for Venetian glass, the haphazard, hit-or-miss methods of the time were accompanied by a proportion of unavoidable failures. Sometimes glass was prepared having an excess of alkali or having the balance of its composition otherwise upset, with the result that it turned out "diseased." One form of diseased glass, sometimes referred to as crizzelled, develops a fine network of minute cracks on its surface. In the most serious cases the glass acquires a sugary texture and completely loses its transparency. Both are forms of deterioration or decomposition of the glass, a state which is hastened by the presence of moisture or high humidity. When an alkali is used greatly in excess of its proper proportion, water glass, which we use for pickling eggs, is the result.

Glass, by the way, is not indestructible. If it is buried in the ground long enough, the surface may be penetrated by moisture in the soil combining with carbon dioxide to form carbonic acid which attacks the alkaline constituent of the glass, causing it to decompose. The oftentimes vividly colored iridescence we see on ancient glasses that have been buried is the result of this action.

Yet in the days before scientific technique gave glassmakers the certainty of always producing consistent quality, the wonder is not that there were failures, but that the glass made then was so good. Were the discoveries of formulae and processes made by the ancients the result of accident, divination, or reason? Who can tell? At the most we may guess that all three contributed, but precisely how or when or where remains a mystery.

At school you were taught that the discovery of glass was an accident. Some Phoenician sailors, you remember, landed on a sandy beach and began cooking a meal, using as a pot rest some lumps of natron, which is a natural carbonate of soda. When the fire was burned out some glass was found among the ashes, the heat having effected the fusion of the silica of the sand and the natron. If you were well taught, you will know that it was Pliny who said so and that the incident took place at the mouth of the River Belus in Syria.

It is an attractive, even a plausible story, but no expert today will agree with it. Some maintain that the heat of a picnic fire is insufficient to produce such a result, others that Egypt is more likely to be one of the lands of origin, because many of the oldest specimens of glass have been found there. For all that, Pliny may have been right in saying that the discovery was accidental and that natron had something to do with it even if he were mistaken about the place and circumstances, for there are deposits of natron in Egypt.

Natron was probably used by the Egyptians throughout their history of glassmaking, and the same type of alkali no doubt came into common use throughout the Near East, Syria, and Greece and Rome, as well, though soda ash obtained from seaweed and inland plants might also have been used. During the Renaissance, Spain exported barilla, made from seaweed, for glassmaking. In the Mediterranean a similar soda was known as *roquetta* and in England as glasswort. Scottish glassmakers, during the seventeenth century and later, obtained a soda ash by piling kelp, a form of seaweed, into stacks and burning it to obtain kelp ash, an alkali.

During the Middle Ages and the Renaissance, glassmakers working far inland used as an alkali a potash made from the ash of burnt bracken, briar, beechwood, or oak. The famous *Waldglas* of Germany and the *verre de fougère* of France were made in this way. These were the usual ways of obtaining alkali in the past, but, since the middle of the nineteenth century, glassmakers have been able to obtain supplies of alkalies from manufacturing chemists.

Although silica for glassmaking usually came from the seashore or river beds, in England during the latter part of the seventeenth century, calcined flint was at first used to make the new lead glass perfected about 1675 by George Ravenscroft. Later it was discovered that sand was equally suitable and, as flint had to be crushed and ground to a powder, sand was cheaper. The term flint, nevertheless, continued to be used to designate a good quality, colorless glass of lead and continues today, along with the loosely used term "crystal," to be applied to such glass. The addition of a large proportion of red lead to the batch, instead of lime, resulted in a soft glass of great brilliance. Indeed, it was a tremendous advance in glass technology that opened the way to new forms of artistic expression, including the fine cutting of the eighteenth century. Other important developments in the history of glass also took place in the seventeenth century. It was then that German workmen developed the heavy potash-chalk glass which made possible the perfection of the engraving techniques introduced there to the glass decorator's repertoire almost a century earlier. It is this glass which is often referred to—again, loosely—as Bohemian "crystal."

In the nineteenth century, machines, particularly in the United States, brought about the greatest revolution in glassmaking technique since the invention of the blowpipe two thousand years ago, thereby extending the use of glass to many departments of life and adding considerably to the material comfort and power of mankind. This change, however, has had only an incidental influence on the artistic side of the craft, if it has had any influence at all.

That is not to say that machine-made articles are necessarily bad in the artistic sense. Indeed, a machine-made object that is designed purely for use, which makes no pretense of artistic effect, is always more pleasing and fundamentally more "artistic" than the overdone elaboration of a hand craftsman too consciously demonstrating his art.

But machine production is different. In it design is a separate function. The designer creates on paper, and the machine carries out his ideas with blind precision. In handwork the craftsman interprets the designer's ideas and, in the process, modifies—indeed, is bound to modify—the original design, for his own individuality intervenes in spite of himself. It is such marks of personality, even when these are slight imperfections, in which is one of the attractions of handmade glass and in which rests its superiority in the artistic field. In any case the subject under discussion is *Old Glass*, and machine production, as they say in the nursery, is another story; therefore, let us pass on.

THE MODERN GLASSHOUSE

As the tools and procedure of glassmaking have altered very little in the last two thousand years, collectors should try at some time to visit a modern glasshouse where handmade glass is being made. Such a visit will show him how pieces have been made in the past and enable him to assess the subtleties of craftsmanship.

In a modern glasshouse the contrast between scientific technique and ancient usage is one of the fascinating features of the place. The furnace, which is scientifically built and controlled, is circular in shape, having perhaps ten pot-openings that glow in the surrounding darkness. Standing by the furnace one may see a glassmaker with a pontil[1] in his hand and a tub at his side in which are the few simple tools of his craft that have hardly changed since the Christian era began. Here the formulae of applied science rules in one section, the craftsman's sleight-of-hand and judgment of eye in the other, and while each retains its individuality, each is a complement of the other.

The floor space is kept clear to allow workers to move easily and give them room to swing the globes of hot glass attached to their blowpipes. In the dimness of the factory, the glare from the furnace doors and the glow from the spheres of hot glass cast the surrounding scene into theatrical highlights, giving the place an air of mystery, a feeling that brings one close to the spirit of a craft that reaches back into ancient times. For an instant a group of solemn, intent, sweat-beaded faces appears and as quickly vanishes,

[1] A pontil, sometimes called a pontee, is an iron rod to which a partly made vessel may be transferred from the blowpipe.

and in that brief instant one realizes that the glassworkers of Alexandria or Sidon must have looked just like that two thousand years ago, for the routine of the craft and its methods have changed very little in all that time.

The craftsmen work in groups called "chairs," although this word is also used for the actual chair in which the leader or "workman" sits (*Plate 1*). A chair may consist of a footmaker, servitor, and workman. (In the past he was usually called the gaffer.) One of the craftsmen dips his blowpipe into the pot of molten metal, gives it a twist or two and brings it out with a blob of molten glass, called a gather, stuck to the end of it. He rolls the gather on a marver (*Plate 2*), a smooth steel plate, although, as the name suggests, marble slabs were used for this purpose long ago, to make it symetrical. He then blows through the blowpipe to inflate the gather slightly, which is then called a parison. After re-heating the paraison, he blows into the blowpipe again, expanding the paraison into a globular or pear-shaped form (*Plate 1*). If he holds the tube above his head when he blows into it, the shape of the globe is spherical; if he allows the tube to hang downward the globe becomes pear-shaped. In its soft, plastic state the globe tends to sag to one side or the other, and he keeps spinning it to preserve balance of form.

The tube is now handed to the workman who sits in the chair, which has two long, wooden arms. He places the tube across the arms and keeps rolling it to and fro with the palm of one hand while, with the other hand, he holds a tool against the spinning globe to give it form. In a few seconds one sees a vase or a bowl taking shape. All this is done almost as quickly as you read these words and certainly in a much shorter time than it takes to write them.

A wineglass is usually made in three parts. After the bowl has been wrought, a blob of glass is stuck to the end of it and drawn and shaped into a stem. A second small blob, or gather, of glass is brought by an assistant and dropped onto the end of the stem (*Plate 3*), then fashioned into a foot by manipulation and centrifugal force. Sometimes a wineglass is made by two craftsmen separately. While the workman makes the bowl, the footmaker is making the stem and foot.

When a piece takes some time to fashion, it begins to cool, and must be re-heated to bring it back to a plastic and workable

Plate I WORKMAN IN "THE CHAIR"
A workman sitting in the chair blowing a sphere of glass. The chair has extended arms across which he will place the blowpipe, spinning it to and fro along the arms. Against the spinning globe of glass he will hold a tool to give it shape.
[*The Central Press Photos Ltd.*]

Plate 2
A gather of glass being rolled on a steel plate to make it symmetrical, preparatory to blowing. [*The Central Press Photos Ltd.*]

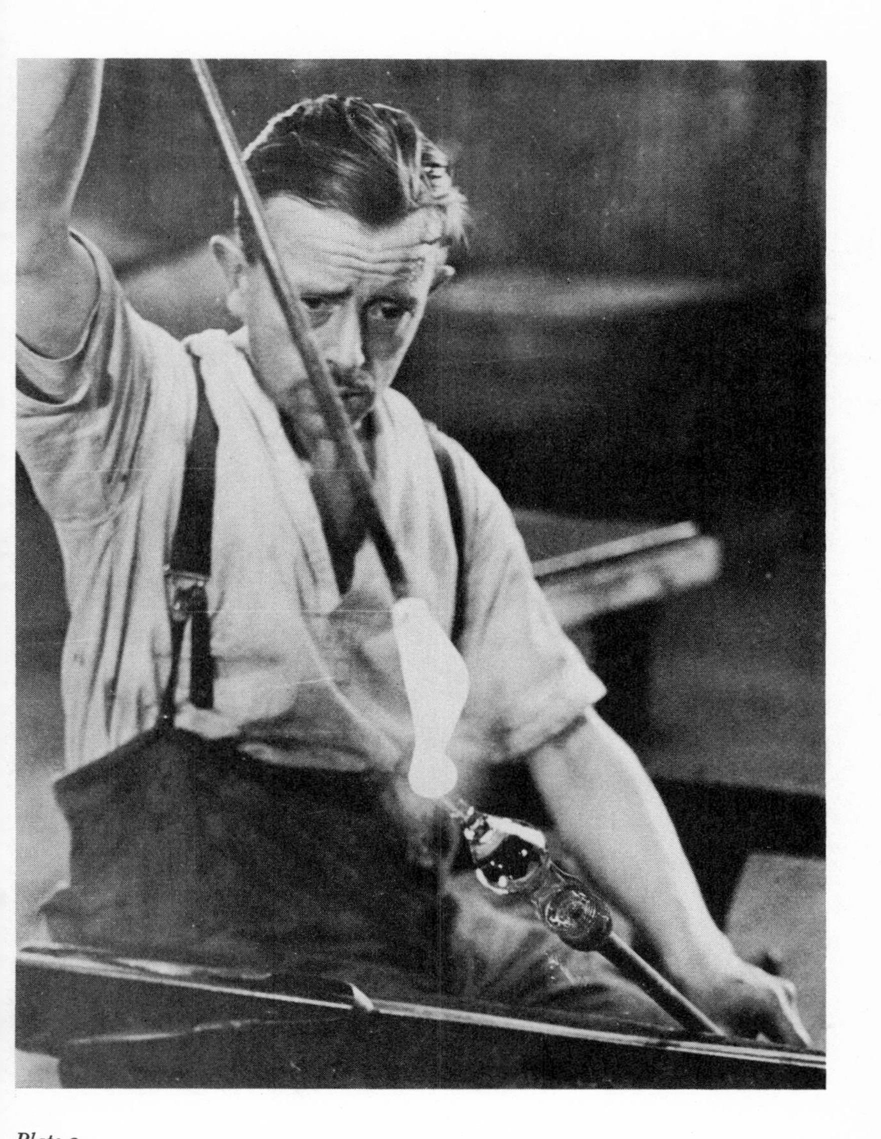

Plate 3
Attaching a blob of glass to a wineglass. This will be fashioned into a foot. Note that the wineglass is attached to the blowpipe by the overblow. This will be cut away at a later stage. [*The Central Press Photos Ltd.*]

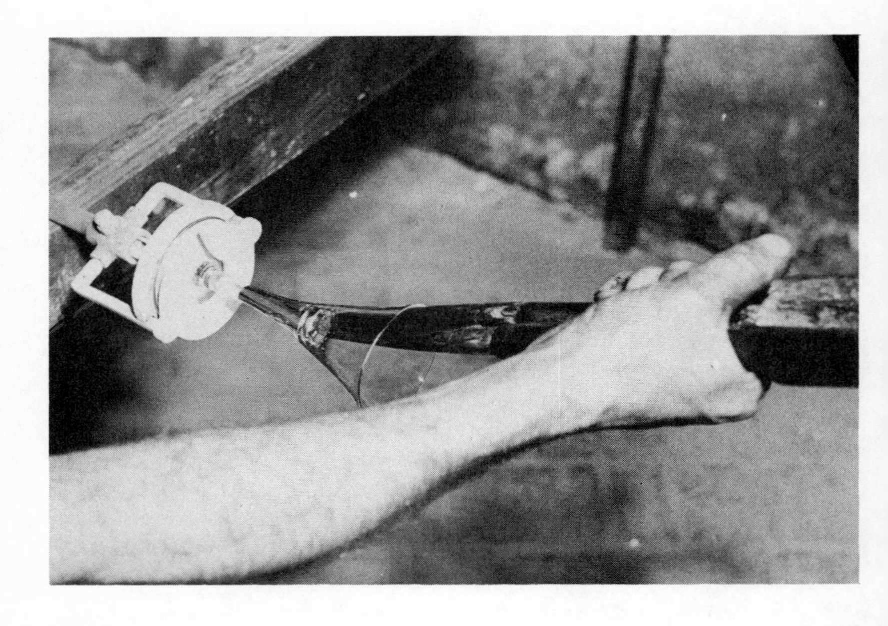

Plate 4
Shearing the rim of a vase. Glass in its plastic state can be readily manipulated and cut with shears. [*The Central Press Photos Ltd.*]

temperature. This is usually done at a small furnace called the glory-hole, but is sometimes also done at the pot-mouth of the melting furnace. The repetition of this process imparts the finish called "fire polish."

When a wineglass, a pitcher or the like is to be completed by hand, it is necessary to hold the base of the piece in some manner in order to shear the rim (*Plate 4*), or otherwise finish the top of the vessel. This is done in several ways: by "sticking it up" by attaching a solid iron rod called a pontil, or pontee, having a small gather of glass on it to the base of the piece; or by using a snap (*Plate 5*), or a snap cup to hold its foot. If an article is to be finished by machine, as is often the case today, it is cracked off from the blowpipe at a point higher than its edge will be when finished, and at a later stage in the manufacture, the overblow, or excess portion that attached the article to the blowpipe during the formative stages, is cut off on a "cracking-off" machine and the edges are ground, polished, or heat finished.

After a piece has been finished it is cracked off from the pontil, or blowpipe, and placed in an annealing oven, called a lehr. Today, this is a long brick-lined steel tunnel through which an iron grid conveying the glass slowly travels. An article placed on the grid at one end comes out of the lehr at the other some hours later, by which time it has been very gradually cooled.

This annealing process is essential and has the effect of preventing internal strains. Glass suddenly cooled is liable to crack and, indeed, if annealing has been scamped, a piece may shiver into pieces without warning, long after it has cooled.

It will be seen that a glass object is the work of several craftsmen working together, and while the leader or workman gives the article its shape, he cannot do so alone but depends on the assistance of others. Good glass, therefore, is only possible where a good team spirit exists. The work requires great dexterity, exact control of hand, and nice judgment of eye. But to those who master the art it becomes an absorbing vocation.

DECORATION

The decoration of glass is done in many different ways, each having many varieties of expression. It may be done by color at the first stage when the metal is in the pot, or it may be applied by the workman when the glass is in its plastic state. Again, decoration may be applied after the article has been made, by cutting or by engraving with a diamond point or by engraving under a wheel. It may be etched by an acid or treated by a sand-blast process. Colors, too, in the form of metallic oxides may be applied. In this process the article, after it has been painted, is placed in a kiln and heated to a temperature just short of melting point. At this point, fusion of the metallic oxides and the glass occurs, so that the colors become an inseparable part of the article so treated. Stained glass artists use this process to fix the painting of features, folds of drapery, and so on into the glass.

The decoration applied by glassmakers in the past shows great ingenuity and superb craftsmanship. A favorite form was applied or "trailed" decoration, achieved by trailing a thread of hot glass on the surface of the vessel, to which it fused. Such trailing sometimes took the form of a spiral around the neck or body of a piece, vertical ribs, or concentric circles which were sometimes pinched together to form "nipt-diamond-waies." In addition, rather abstract designs as well as imaginative birds and animals were forms of trailed decoration. Often these designs were further embellished by being marked by a wheel having a pattern of parallel notches on its face, making "rigaree" trails.

The delicate filigree in the stems of some English eighteenth-century wineglasses was produced by arranging a series of opaque white rods of glass, called canes, around the side of a ribbed mold, then inserting a gather of colorless glass on the end of a blowpipe or pontil into it to pick up the canes. Gather and canes were then reheated and marvered so they would be well fused, then another gather of colorless glass was made over them, and the whole mass again marvered and tooled to the desired size of the stem which was then added to the bowl of the wineglass. By varying the arrangement and color of the canes in the mold and twisting the final gather, a wide variety of spiral patterns was achieved. This technique, used to make hollow vessels, was brought to a high degree of perfection by the Venetians in the sixteenth and seventeenth centuries, and is called *latticinio*.

Another favorite English design applied to wineglasses was the "air twist." To make this, several bubbles of air were entrapped in the base of the wineglass which was then pulled and twisted to form the stem. The pulling elongated the teardrop-shaped air

Plate 5

Opening out the bowl of a wineglass being turned backwards and forwards across the arms of the chair. The foot of the glass is held by a spring tool called a snap, which does not leave a pontil-mark on the base of the piece.

[*The Central Press Photos Ltd.*]

Plate 6
Tubes or rods called "canes" are made by two workers, each with an iron rod attached to the same blob of glass. They walk off in opposite directions and pull the glass until it is the desired thickness. The illustration shows the making of thermometer tubes. [*The Central Press Photos Ltd.*]

Plate 7 GLASS CUTTING
A craftsman cutting glass. Note that the vase is held above the wheel, not under it as is the case in wheel engraving. [*Edinburgh & Leith Flint Glass Co., Ltd.*]

Plate 8 ENGRAVER'S LATHE
An engraver at work at Steuben Glass, Corning, New York. The rack holds a great variety of copper discs used in the process. A mixture of oil and abrasive powder drips from the pointed brass plate onto the edge of the copper disc, thereby giving the edge of the disc the property of a little grindstone. [*Steuben Glass*]

bubbles so that they became slender air tubes, which became spirals when the stem was twisted. In some cases the air twist stems were made apart from the bowl, then attached to it. An endless variety of patterns could be achieved by varying the number and placement of the air bubbles. Indeed, the variety of decoration possible when glass is in a plastic state is very wide, and one can only wonder at the amazing skill that was able to produce so many fine and sophisticated effects with nothing to aid it but pincers, tongs, and a few primitive tools.

Glass cutting at one time was done by a cast-iron wheel on the edge of which trickled a mixture of water and abrasive powder. Today, however, a carborundum grindstone is often used. This has a V-shaped edge, although flat- or round-edged stones are used for special effects (*Plate 7*).

Usually cut glass designs are geometric, and in the first stage a girl paints a number of vertical lines on the piece to be cut, for the guidance of the cutter. In the case of a vase these lines may divide the surface into five sections, and in one of these sections she paints a few lines forming one or two angles. This is to help the cutter to start the design, and since no further guidance is given him, the result is dependent upon his judgment and skill.

The cutter holds the piece above the revolving stone and, by turning it to and fro, cuts the design with amazing rapidity and sureness. Each facet must be rough cut on a coarse carborundum or iron wheel with coarse emery powder, smoothed on a stone wheel, then polished on a wooden or felt wheel with the aid of tin oxide, or a similar agent. Considering that he has only a few lines to guide him and that these give only a hint of the pattern he is to make, it is surprising to see a complicated design taking shape so quickly and with such precision. The feat is all the more wonderful when it is considered that he has to hold a heavy object and move it about over a revolving wheel without the assistance of a rest against which he may steady the work or support his own arms.

The delicate art of wheel engraving is done by an engraver's lathe. This is simply a revolving disc of copper (*Plate 8*) to the edge of which emery powder mixed in oil is applied, so that the disc is in effect a little grindstone. The piece of glass being engraved is held against the revolving disc and moved about freehand, a process requiring a far higher degree of skill, but giving a wider scope for expression, than engraving done with a diamond point. To obtain different effects the copper disc is changed from time to time. Some of the discs have V-shaped edges, some have round edges, some are small as a pinhead, some as big as a silver dollar, and all vary in thickness.

Engraving done in this way can achieve marvels of intricate and minute detail. For that reason the art requires in its executants not only a high degree of skill, but what is often more difficult to find, restraint and good taste. Furthermore, there must be a feeling for the nature of the medium and a sense of the suitability of design. The engraver, in fact, must be an artist. But such work, when done by a master, is the most charming and delicate of all the arts expressed through glass; and it certainly is the most neglected and most overlooked.

This account of the nature of glass and how it is fashioned and how decorated is necessarily brief. It attempts no more than an outline of the subject, yet it will suffice to give that background of knowledge without which the following history must lose much of its significance, and the achievements of the great craftsmen of the past be only faintly realized.

Chapter Two

EGYPTIAN AND ROMAN GLASS

EGYPTIAN GLASS

UNTIL the invention of the blowpipe sometime in the first century B.C., glass was produced in very limited quantities. Though highly prized by those few to whom it was available, it was most often used to imitate precious or semi-precious stones, or vessels of other materials, and many of its unique characteristics were not appreciated or exploited.

The many-sided character of glass became ever more evident as the material was gradually developed over a long span of years. Its evolution can probably be first traced as a glaze for beads of stone or ceramic into beads of solid glass by at least 1500 B.C. So far as we know today, it was also at about this time that glass seems to have been first fashioned into small vessels of various forms similar to those of stone and ceramics. This development seems to have occurred simultaneously in Egypt and other areas of the Near East. These vessels, however, were expensive and quite beyond the reach of the poor or even middle class of that time, so that interest in glass as an art belonged to an exclusive circle. Its universal application, which we take so much for granted today, was a thing unknown.

Only a relatively few contemporary references from this early period of the development of glass are as yet known to us. What we know of its nature and use has been largely the result of the work of archaeologists. There are many gaps in the sequence of the story which may remain for some time to come, and perhaps forever. Subsequent discoveries, of course, may affirm or refute what is conjectural, and will undoubtedly add to our knowledge, but it is possible that the whole story will never be written, and with that we must be content.

Fortunately, the pagan practice of taking collections of household goods to the grave included glass vessels, and from the tombs of ancient kings many fine specimens have come to us whose age can be fairly accurately ascertained. And from the remains of glassmakers' crucibles and partly manufactured glass dug up at Tell el-Amarna and other places, ancient processes and techniques have been revealed. Finds of the kind are by no means rare and form sufficient evidence upon which to construct a historical account approximating the truth.

For many years it has generally been supposed that glass was first made in the region of the Nile Delta, although Syria has also been claimed as the land of origin. There seems to be little evidence to support the Syrian claim, but recent discoveries of intricate mosaic glasses found at sites in northwestern Iran, but which were likely made in a Mesopotamian glassmaking center, point to a highly developed and sophisticated glassmaking technology there which offers a challenge to those who claim Egypt as the birthplace of glass. When the discovery of glass was made is yet unknown, but beads of glazed stone or faience were apparently made as far back as 3000 B.C.

Doubtless glass would be used in this way first of all, and doubtless it had commercial value as a medium of exchange with primitive peoples living beyond the frontiers of civilization. Later it would be seen that a bead might as well be made of solid glass. Today we are accustomed to think of transparency as the outstanding characteristic of glass, but in its early beginnings this was not at all obvious and even its potential as a transparent metal was not evident. It was always made in colors, which were sometimes translucent but most often opaque, and its chief attraction was that it could be made to resemble precious or semi-precious stones which could be cut by the lapidary.

A long period passed before glass was fashioned into vessels, but during that time a preoccupation in the art of imitating precious stones resulted in the achievement of a color technology of the first rank. When the time came to make vessels, this technology was apparently firmly established, for the shades of dark blue, turquoise, and yellow of the early period have perhaps never been equaled since. The earliest vessels of any artistic worth were made about 1500 B.C., and although these represent an art less fully developed than is to be seen in the specimens produced during the reign of Amenhotep II, sixty years later, they are by no means immature, and the inference that a long experimental period may have passed before such a result is possible is justified.

The technique used in making vessels at this time was simple but was one that demanded a high degree of skill. One theory is that, first of all, a core of some material such as sand and clay was formed to the shape desired around the end of a copper or bronze rod. The rod projected and served as a handle for the craftsman. The core was heated, then molten glass melted in a crucible in a small furnace was probably pulled from the crucible in the form of a thread or trail by means of another hooked metal rod. As the core was rotated the thread was wound closely around it until it was completely covered. This process was repeated, with numerous re-heatings and marverings, until the vessel reached the desired form and thickness.

Decoration was applied by adding threads of hot glass of different colors to the surface and working these into it, combing them into feathered or palmette patterns, or some other conventional design. Handles were also applied, usually of a different colored glass from the body of the vessel (*Plate 9*).

When the piece had been annealed, the metal rod was removed, the core dug out to form the rather rough, hollow interior of the vessel and the exterior may sometimes have been ground and polished to finish it. Specimens of this period are to be seen in the British and the Victoria and Albert Museums, the Metropolitan and Toledo Museums of Art, and the Corning Museum of Glass, as well as elsewhere in collections of ancient art. The quality of the glass made then is first rate, the colors, which are opaque as a rule, are subtle and the craftsmanship superb.

In this early period glass was also being used to a limited extent for mosaic. Another technique that developed about that same time was the production of glass objects cast, or press-cast, in a mold. In some instances the glass in its plastic state may have been pressed into the mold, but in most cases glass paste, made by grinding frit to a powder, was used. Frit is partially made glass in which the process of fusion has not been completed. The period, indeed, was one of discovery and advance, yet, even so, the possibilities of the medium were hardly touched.

The art flourished for some time after this glorious period, but gradually began to lose impetus, and a hiatus seems to have occurred in Egyptian glassmaking between the thirteenth and fourth centuries B.C. Glassmaking, however, continued in Mesopotamia during this period. In Mesopotamia, vessels made by the core process like those in Egypt, but usually of less colorful glass, were produced, including a vase now in the British Museum on which is engraved the name of Sargon, King of Assyria. To the ordinary man of our time the name means little, but it may not be without interest to know that the vase was once owned by the same Sargon, the king of kings, who has been portrayed for us by H. G. Wells in his novel *Christina Alberta's Father*, and who exerted such a disconcerting influence on an English middle-class family of the twentieth century.

In any case, when Egypt gained independence, there was a revival of the arts, including glass. This seems to have been a national movement undertaken in much the same spirit in which William Morris reclaimed the arts of the Middle Ages. The glass of this time is imitative and follows the patterns and designs of the fifteenth-century period, but it does not equal the original either in quality or color. Nevertheless it was a fresh start, and from this point the art continued without serious interruption, building up a tradition that was to make Alexandria supreme when the invention of the blowpipe opened a new phase of far wider possibilities.

It may be felt that any advance in glassmaking made by the Egyptians was slight when one considers that the craft was practiced by them for several centuries. This tardy development may be accounted for to some extent by the conservatism for which Egyptian craftsmen were notorious, but it should be remembered that no great advance was possible until the blowpipe had been invented, and that this invention, simple as it is, was by no means obvious. Certainly, glassmaking at that time was limited in scope in Egypt, but it was also elsewhere in the Near East where it was practiced. What Egyptians gave to the art was a color technology and a tradition upon which the new era could build, and this was by no means an inconsiderable contribution.

Plate 9
Egyptian core-wound vessel, probably fifteenth or fourteenth century B.C.
[*Victoria and Albert Museum photograph. Crown Copyright*]

Plate 10 ROMAN GLASS
A pillar molded bowl, probably made in Alexandria during the first century A.D.
[*Victoria and Albert Museum photograph. Crown Copyright*]

ROMAN GLASS

The term Roman glass does not refer to glass made only in Rome, but is applied to all glass made within the Roman Empire. Thus glass made in Alexandria and Sidon, the two great glass-making centers in the world at the time when the Roman Empire was established, come within this category, which is, in fact, a classification by time rather than by style. Experts make a further subdivision of this classification by using the terms Roman I and Roman II. Roman I indicates glass made during the first two centuries A.D., and Roman II glass made in the third and fourth centuries.

But classification by style is also useful. The two schools at that time were Alexandrian and Syrian. Alexandrian designs were stylized and traditional, Syrian designs naturalistic, with a touch of impressionism in their execution; Alexandrian glass was heavy, Syrian glass thin; Alexandrian glass had subtlety of color and was of excellent quality, Syrian glass was less concerned either with color or quality; and Syrian glass as a rule has a pale blue-green color, although at a later period an attractive honey yellow was produced.

Just before the blowpipe was invented, glassmaking flourished in Alexandria and Sidon with great vigor, and it may be that this phase of renewed vitality created the conditions to make that invention possible. In Alexandria at that time a luxury trade in bowls was in full swing (*Plate 10*). It is not exactly known how bowls of this type were made, but they form a distinct class of early Roman glass. They may have been press-molded, and are evidently finished by cutting and polishing. Deep blue and amethyst, as well as greenish, amber, and honey-colored examples are known.

Sometimes bowls were made of a number of small pieces of glass of different colors placed together like a mosaic around the inside of a mold of the form desired. A core of the same form, but somewhat smaller, was then set in place and the whole heated in a small furnace until the glass was fused. After annealing, the piece was finished by cutting and polishing. These are sometimes held to be the murrine bowls of antiquity, but of that there is more than a little doubt. It is difficult to find a satisfactory definition of this word, for ancient writers themselves are at variance, but murrine is usually accepted as meaning a bowl made in a mosaic of precious or semi-precious stones such as agate or sardonyx. The glass mosaic bowls were very likely an imitation of this sort of thing. Indeed, some of them were more than an imitation and were, in fact, actual fakes. At least such an eminent authority as W. A. Thorpe says so when he writes in his book, *English Glass*:

> Murrine was an Oriental dealers' word and rather like "opal" in the modern glass trade. It was a rough-and-ready shop category. It meant fancy goods, cups and the like, made of ringed and streaky stones, precious or semi-precious, and cheaper imitations made of many colored glass. That is why Roman writers describe it so differently and were so often taken in by fakes. In 61 B.C. an exhibition was held in the temple of Jupiter Capitolinus of stone murrines (cups and bowls), brought home by Pompey and other military men from the war in the East. They created a sensation. The Alexandrian glass manufacturers snapped on to it and flooded the market with fakes in a year or two.

The Victoria and Albert Museum and the Metropolitan Museum, as well as others, contain some exceptionally fine specimens of this kind of glass, including some of the type known as *millefiori* (*Plate 11c*). In this case the small pieces of glass of which the mosaic is composed are in the shape of rosettes and thus anticipate the *millefiori* for which France was renowned in the nineteenth century. Bowls of mosaic glass were often decorated with vertical ribs called "pillar molding" (*Plate 10*). This decoration was formed in the mold and is an integral part of the bowl, not an applied decoration. An additional decoration often found on *millefiori* bowls consists of a rope twist around the rim. This was sometimes of clear glass in which were embedded opaque white twisted canes, in the manner of the Venetian *latticinio*, which it anticipated by some sixteen centuries.

EARLY TECHNIQUES

The precise date of the invention of the blowpipe is unknown, but it is generally believed to have taken place in the second half of the first century B.C. Neither is it known where the invention was made, but there is some evidence to suggest it may have been Syria, possibly at Sidon.

It is not known whether the first blown glass was free-blown, or blown in a mold. From accurately dated examples we know that if not used initially, molds were used almost immediately after the discovery of the blowpipe. A mold is made of two or more vertical sections that, when closed, become a hollow container of the shape of the vessel to be blown, often bearing a design incised on its interior walls. The glassblower places the paraison of hot glass at the end of his blowpipe into the mold and, blowing through the pipe, inflates the bubble of glass until it completely fills the mold, taking its shape and design. The mold is then opened and the completed vessel removed, ready to be "stuck-up" with a pontil so its mouth can be finished. The use of a mold enables the glass-worker to turn out identical glass articles in surprising quantities. The earliest molds used in Sidon and elsewhere may have been made of ceramic, but it seems likely, in view of the developed technology of metalwork of the period, that they would have soon given way to metal ones. The mold-blown technique is still in use today by glassworkers, and has also been adapted to high-speed machine production.

Both techniques of free-blown and mold-blown glass were well established by the first century A.D., so that glass as a common commodity came within reach of a public far greater than had hitherto been possible. Molds assured repetitive pieces of identical shape, size, and design: free-blowing permitted the glass artist to express himself in a great variety of ways, both by manipulating the glass and applying ornament to it while in its plastic state, and by cutting or engraving after the glass had been made (*Plate 11*).

The immediate effect of the invention of the blowpipe was to make glass accessible to everyone and to add greatly to the convenience of mankind by supplying vessels for the storage of all sorts of liquids, and by providing dishes and cups and other domestic utensils cheaply and in quantities. This was followed by the manufacture of window glass, of mirrors and even lenses. In the artistic field the invention broke the bonds that had held the art within the prison of mere imitation and substitution, and opened up a wide prospect of new and exciting possibilities.

This new and invigorating impetus to the craft was accompanied by the spread of glassmaking from its traditional centers of Alexandria and Sidon to every province within the Roman Empire. From Syria to Cologne the Roman Army ruled over the barbaric nations and rude tribes that peopled Asia and Europe at that time, giving law and that security without which trade dwindles and dies, learning becomes obstructed, and art is eclipsed.

As it happened, the necessities of the expanding industry and the character of the workmen themselves exploited this favorable state of affairs to the full, so that glassmaking became widespread and so firmly established that not even the fall of the Roman Empire and the Dark Ages that followed were able to bring about its complete dissolution. And thus, despite all the calamities and upheavals throughout Europe's stormy history, the craft reaches our time in a line of unbroken continuity.

Because it is fragile, glass is difficult to transport, and it was easier in these early days for glassmakers to come to the centers of civilization, and there set up the simple apparatus of their glass-houses, than to distribute their wares from a distant place. Furthermore, glassmaking requires an abundance of fuel, and this circumstance often forced glassmakers to move to other districts when they had exhausted the supplies available to them. Perhaps these conditions affected the character of the workmen themselves, for they were apparently restless in spirit, and seemed to prefer an itinerant life to a settled existence in one place.

This attitude of mind produced independence and with it a touchy pride that made dealing with them rather trying to others. These peculiarities remained with them even into modern times. The expensive and elaborate plant usual in an industrial and complex society cannot, of course, be moved about at the whim of a workman, but at least the workmen themselves are free to change masters; and this they did in the same unsettled way of their ancient forerunners even as late as mid-Victorian times.

Before the first century A.D. had closed, glassmaking was practiced in every part of the Roman Empire. Alexandria and Sidon (*Plate 12*) still retained their reputation, but glass hardly inferior to the products of these ancient and traditional centers was being produced as far north as Cologne. In Italy, glassmaking existed on the Campanian coast and in Rome itself. In England, glass was being made near Warrington, in Northamptonshire, and at Colchester; and in Gaul (*Plate 13*) the industry became established in the Moselle valley. By the third century Northern glass had reached its best period. The craftsmen in Europe at that time were mostly Syrian and Egyptian, men who had traveled far from home, impelled by a natural love of wandering or the hope of

a

b

c

Plate II THE ROMAN PERIODS I AND II

a Vase of green glass from Mount Carmel. Fourth century A.D. Height 3 inches.
b Vase of pale bluish-green glass. Applied trails in merrythought or wishbone pattern. From Mount Carmel. Fourth–fifth century A.D. Height 3¼ inches.
c Bowl of *millefiori* glass. First century A.D.

[*The Royal Scottish Museum, Edinburgh*]

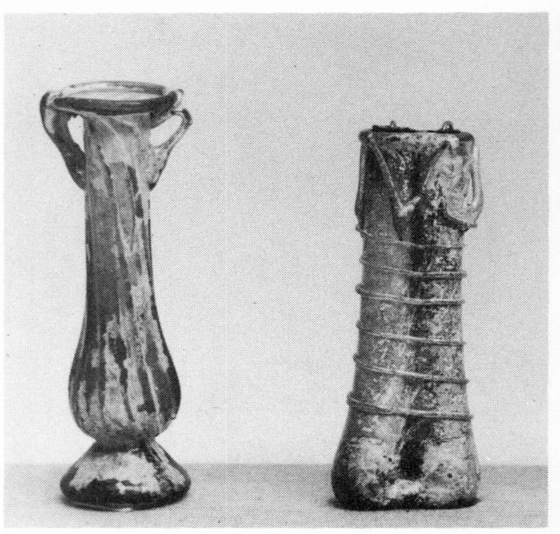

a, b

c, d, e

Plate 12 SYRIAN GLASS OF THE ROMAN PERIOD

a Phial of honey-colored glass, from Mount Carmel. Third–fourth century A.D.

b Double phial ornamented with applied thread, from Mount Carmel. Third–fourth century A.D.

c Phial with open zigzag fillets from lip to shoulder. From Mount Carmel. Third–fourth century A.D.

d Phial of greenish glass, bow handle and wavy fillets on body. From Sidon. Third–fourth century A.D.

e Amphora with trail applied to body in wishbone pattern. From Hebron. Third century A.D.

[*The Royal Scottish Museum, Edinburgh*]

a

b

c

Plate 13 ROMAN GLASS

a From Gaul, third or fourth century.

b From Abbeville, first or second century.

c From Amiens, second or third century.

[*Victoria and Albert Museum photograph. Crown Copyright*]

Plate 14 MOLD-BLOWN GLASS

Large amber pitcher, signed underneath the handle "Ennion made it"—the most famous ancient glassmaker known. Probably made in Sidon about early first century A.D. The small bottle of opaque white glass is probably from Sidon about the same time. [*The Corning Museum of Glass*] gain. For this reason Roman glass has no distinct national styles and it is not always easy to ascribe the land of origin of a piece with certainty. But one thing we can be sure of and that is that glass, before the first century had closed, had become a common trade commodity.

The date of origin of a piece is often determined from objects found in graves, but, in most cases, such a method cannot be precise and must be accepted within broad limits. The glass found among the ruins of Pompeii, too, has provided much reliable information, and the practice of the early makers molding their names on the pieces they manufactured has also been useful. Of these Ennion (*Plate 14*), who began in Sidon and worked for a while in Italy, Artas of Sidon, and Frontinus, who worked at Boulogne or Amiens, are the best known. Other makers were Jason, Megas, and Neikaios. Sometimes a name was accompanied with a puff or advertisement, one of which might be freely translated as:

"Made by Jason—Don't forget it."

As we have seen, a glass object cannot be made by a single craftsman alone, but is always the result of a team of workmen, or, it may be, of several different teams, each contributing a highly specialized skill. First is the making of the metal, then comes the blowing and shaping of the glass, then the decoration applied by the glassmaker during the formative stages or by the etcher or engraver when the article has been made.

Of decoration applied by the glassmaker the trail was the most natural. The Syrians used this form, but it had much greater popularity in the northern part of the Empire where it became more fully developed. Trails were applied vertically or horizontally or in spirals. When a trail was applied to a very hot glass it became almost absorbed by the body of the vessel, or an opposite effect was obtained by working the trail with pincers and bringing it up in bold relief. Parallel trails were sometimes drawn together at intervals to form a diamond pattern, or what Ravenscroft, the great English glassmaker of the seventeenth century, called "nipt-diamond-waies" (*Plate 15*). In the third century a similar treatment was given handles to make what is known as the "chain handle," which is in effect two separate handles drawn together and joined at various intervals.

Rich effects were sometimes obtained by using trails of a different color from the vessel they adorned. Another type of contrasting color decoration was made by drops of glass placed over the surface. An amber vessel, for example, might have green spots. Work of this kind was done in Egypt, and the Rhineland as well. And so, by the application of trails, by contrasting colors, by stamping, nipping, and other manipulation, decoration by the glassworker was both varied and wide in scope.

It cannot be said that all Roman glass was executed with faultless taste. In the later period particularly, when the simplicity and restraint of the early period had given place to a more fanciful execution, decoration was often excessive and overdone. In the later period, too, less importance was attached to the quality of the actual metal, which diminished in purity as time went on. Nevertheless, the first four centuries was a period of great vitality and technical advance.

The visitor to museums may be struck by an elusive charm of subtle coloring to be seen in certain Roman glass. This quality, however, was not one imparted by the original creator, but is something that has been acquired by accident. Long burial in damp earth has caused a decay in which the alkali has been drawn from the composition of the glass, changing its texture to a series of layers of iridescence. It is the breaking up of the light prismatically by the broken surface of the glass that produces the attractive color and gives those tints like an opal.

By Roman times glass cutting had become separated from glassmaking, and the terms *diatretarii* refer to glass cutters not attached to a glasshouse and *vitrerii* to glassmakers. Cameo cutting was a branch of glassworking that was brought to a high level of excellence. In this, a layer, or as many as five layers, of colored glass was cased with opaque white glass. Designs in relief were then created by cutting through the layer of white, and other colored layers if they were present, with simple gravers' tools. Very striking and subtle effects were thus created. One of the most famous examples of this technique is a vase once belonging to the Duke of Portland, now in the British Museum (*Plate 16*). Wedgwood's well-known "jasper" stoneware vase is a direct copy of this Roman vase.

In earlier Roman times engraving was used merely to give emphasis to the form of a vessel, and it was, therefore, very

Plate 15 RHINELAND GLASS
Jug or ewer, free-blown of light greenish glass with applied decoration, including "nipt-diamond-waies" and small blue glass prunts. Made in the Cologne area in the second century A.D. Height 16½ inches. [*The Corning Museum of Glass*]

Plate 16 THE PORTLAND VASE
In Roman times cameo relief was a branch of cutting that reached a high stage of development. This superb specimen was a model for Wedgwood when he made "jasper" stoneware. It should be compared with the Northwood Vase, Plate 45. [*British Museum*]

restrained in its treatment. This might be done by cutting a number of horizontal rings round a vase, or applying some other simple design. Indeed, some critics, Ruskin among them, believe glass cutting is only legitimate when applied in this way, and that any type of decoration that covers up the form given by the glassmaker is to be condemned.

In the later period, however, cutting was often carried to extravagant lengths in producing works of great virtuosity. The most outstanding of these are the cups or beakers known today by the term cage-cups. From a thick-walled cup, the glass cutters created a network of fine circles in high relief and free from the solid wall of the cup except for small stubs of glass by which they remain attached to it. An inscription above this network is usually a part of the design, also undercut and left in high relief. In the Rhineland, cutting and engraving continued to be more restrained. Patterns there were often of simple geometric form, especially during the third and fourth centuries A.D.

Applying enamel colors to glass was also done in Roman times, although never very extensively. Another type of decoration, in which the design was scratched or engraved through gold leaf, demands more attention. In this technique gold leaf was applied to a piece of glass, and a design, sometimes a portrait, scratched through the gold. Another piece of glass was then placed over it and the two pieces fused together, thus providing a perfect protection for the gold leaf. This form of decoration was applied to the bases of cups, and bowls, the remains of most of which we know having been found embedded in the walls of tombs in the catacombs. Many of the representations were of individuals or members of a family and bear toasts such as "Drink and be alive," or similar good wishes. Others bear representations of Sts. Peter and Paul (*Plate 17*), the Good Shepherd, and Christian symbols, while numerous gold glasses bear Jewish symbols. It is not known where this technique originated, but since early writings suggest there was a highly developed glassmaking center in Alexandria in the third century B.C., it is possible that it may have been there. Some of the best gold glasses of the third and fourth centuries A.D. were made in the northern part of the Roman Empire. Gold glasses of an entirely different character were also being made at this time in the Sassanian Kingdom of Persia (*Plate 17*).

The study of Roman glass is never beside the point. It is important to the collector in that this early period devised most of the methods used throughout the subsequent history of glass. Furthermore, the craftsmanship of this time does not fall short of the best periods in later days. And certainly, in the artistic field, Roman glass was not without considerable influence on English craftsmanship and design. The ordinary collector, however, is unlikely to come by any ancient glass, except for an occasional tear bottle or some such small fry if he is lucky enough. Yet for him there are always the museum collections, and how splendid many of these can be.

It should be pointed out here, perhaps, that some museums keep all their glass, of every period, in one department, but that others do not. The latter keep ancient glass in a separate place from modern glass, that is from glass of the seventeenth century to the present day. Kelvingrove Art Gallery of Glasgow is a case in point. Here the visitor might see a good collection of modern glass shown in an upper gallery, and leave the building unaware that the archaeological department, on the ground floor, contains some specimens of good Egyptian and Syrian glass of an early period.

GOLD GLASS MEDALLION (*top*)
Gold medallion with portraits of Saints Peter and Paul. The design is in gold leaf laminated between two layers of glass. Probably made in Rome early in the fourth century A.D. Diameter 4 inches. [*The Corning Museum of Glass*]

GOLD GLASS CUP (*bottom*)
Parthian or Sassanian gold glass cup dating from the third and fourth century A.D
[*The Corning Museum of Glass*]

Chapter Three

ISLAMIC GLASS — THE NORTHERN APPEAL

GLASSMAKING IN THE NEAR EAST

WHEN, in the fifth century, Rome lost her grip on the northern frontiers of her empire that were protected by the Rhine and Danube, a period of chaos followed in which Goths, Vandals, Franks, Burgundians, Huns, and lesser predatory tribes swarmed across Europe in savage hordes, dispersing Roman arms and Roman law, fighting among themselves and even sacking Rome itself. In the long, unsettled period that followed, learning was all but extinct and with it the fine arts. It could hardly be otherwise, for this was no conquest of a worn-out civilization by vigorous barbarians in which sophistication and refinement were replaced by a crude but vital culture. It was rather a continuous migration, a series of conquests in which tribes of marauding nomads followed one another, each vanquishing its predecessor, then becoming vanquished in turn by its successor.

Those who had suffered most were not the warriors, but the people of peaceful habits trying to carry on the work of production without which even primitive races cannot survive. To give such valuable social service in those times, however, was to be despised. As for the artist, he had hardly the right to live. Doubtless the futile triviality of his existence was brought home to him in variations of the constantly repeated phrase: "Remember we're at war now," just as he has been similarly taxed by hysterical patriots in an age which, we pride ourselves, is enlightened.

Glass, however, had become more than a medium of artistic expression by this time and was something that supplied a common need. One imagines that its use was too convenient and universal for the craft to become wholly extinguished, and while there is no evidence to show that glass was made in the traditional centers of Italy, southern France, and Catalonia during that period, it is not unlikely that the common utensils were still being produced. But if the craft ever rose above the level of utility, no specimen has come down to us to prove the fact. We cannot be certain that glass was made in Italy during the Lombard occupation, for instance, but we may guess that common glass probably was, and artistic glass was not.

In the North, in northern Gaul and Germany, the situation was rather different. There the Franks had established something that could be called a state and, by the sixth century, an area extending from the North Sea to the Mediterranean enjoyed a somewhat tempered security under their pagan rule. There, in the Seine–Rhine area, glassmaking continued, and there the production of drinking vessels of a new design, having the quality known as "Northern Appeal," gave types as good as anything hitherto known. Before discussing this glass particularly, however, it might be advisable to turn to a richer field and to give an outline of glassmaking as it continued in the East under the influence of Roman civilization.

When the Roman Empire shifted the seat of government from Rome to Byzantium under the rule of Constantine, Roman civilization was to undergo a change, brought about by the impact upon it of Greek traditions and culture. The result was the Greco-Roman civilization known as Byzantine, which had such important cultural influences not only in its own day, but long after the Empire had become one with Nineveh and Tyre. Its importance to the glass collector is in the fact that Syrian and Egyptian glass continued to be made and that the surviving pieces now fill what would otherwise be a period of almost complete emptiness.

The glass in the Near East at this time tended to turn from classical and traditional designs, and it became, indeed, in its ebullient moments, somewhat freakish. No prevailing tendency predominated and it was some time before a recognizable style was produced. Difficulty exists in giving dates for much of this glass, but, thanks to the work of a band of German archaeologists who carried out excavations at Samarra in the years between

SYRIAN MOSQUE LAMP
Enameled; with Arabic inscriptions and chalices and flowers. Mid-fourteenth century A.D.
[*The Royal Scottish Museum, Edinburgh*]

SYRIAN ENAMELED GLASS
A good example from the fourteenth century.
[*Victoria and Albert Museum photograph. Crown Copyright*]

ENAMELED BOTTLE Islamic bottle of light greenish glass enameled and gilt with "endless knot" and fleur-de-lys-like motifs. Probably made in Syria about mid-thirteenth century.
[*The Corning Museum of Glass*]

ISLAMIC CUT BEAKER Free-blown and relief cut; Islamic; Egypt or Persia, ca. tenth century. Height $5\frac{1}{8}$ inches. Almost colorless glass. Beaker is decorated by relief cutting depicting three eagle-like birds, a cufic inscription, and several simple geometric motifs.
[*The Corning Museum of Glass*]

1912 and 1914, exciting finds were made that have been of great value in giving the date of manufacture of a fair range of glass, and doing so with some degree of certainty.

The glass found at Samarra was varied, and ranged from common bottles to fine bowls, apparently of Egyptian origin. Some of these are cut in a stylized decoration and executed with restraint and refinement in the best manner.

The rise of Mohammed had a profound influence on Syrian glassmaking, and Syrian glass after the sixth century loses much of its Semitic flavor and expresses a new idiom so that it has become known as Islamic, a term now used to denote glass made throughout the Arab world. A comparatively large quantity of Islamic glass exists, and that more will be discovered as time goes on is probable. If one may judge from the quantities found in Iraq and Palestine, it is clear that glassmaking was very active in these places.

Specimens of this glass include globular and cylindrical bottles and bowls decorated by trails. In some cases the trails are arranged as a lattice, in others applied to form starfish designs. There are cut bottles, usually square in section, in which the decoration is elaborate.

Different Roman techniques were revived during the Islamic period, too, including painting on glass, although this activity seems to have been exclusively Egyptian. Here, indeed, a new technique was invented whereby glass was stained in different colors. How this was done is unknown; at any rate there has never been a satisfactory explanation of the process. In this group is usually classed glass painted in lusters of which most of the specimens have been found in Egypt.

The art of enameling glass reached a high level of development at this time and found its best expression in Syria (*Plate 18*). Usually the glass used for this purpose was not entirely colorless, but was of a light greenish, brownish or sometimes honey color. Decoration, particularly in the later works of the fourteenth century, takes the form of an overall pattern of finely drawn, stylized, foliate and geometric forms. Earlier examples of Islamic enameled glass are more restrained and do not bear such overall decoration (*Plate 19*). A famous cup, decorated in this way, is to be seen at the Victoria and Albert Museum. It was for many generations in the Musgrave family of Edenhall, near Penrith, and is known by the romantic name of "The Luck of Edenhall." In all likelihood it was brought home by a Crusader towards the end of the fourteenth century. Another fine specimen included in the Slade Collection at the British Museum is a pear-shaped flask which came from the Würzburg family.

By the end of the thirteenth century Damascus had become a glassmaking center, and the specimens of enameled glass from here are exquisite in workmanship and design. In this a strong Chinese influence is apparent and testifies to the existence of a commercial intercourse with the Far East during that time.

Not least among the specimens of Islamic glass must be classed Egyptian mosque lamps. These were hung from the roof by chains. Many of them are treated in enamel in which rich effects have been obtained. Religious symbolism and texts from the Koran were used in the decoration. The biggest collection of these lamps which can be seen in any place outside of Cairo is housed in the Victoria and Albert Museum, but specimens are to be found in many provincial museums as well (*Plate 18*).

Cutting, both incised and in high relief, is another form of glass decoration for which Islamic glassmakers are noted. This art reached great heights between the ninth and twelfth centuries (*Plate 19*). Famous among glasses cut in high, cameo-like relief are the Hedwig beakers, so called because a glass of this type is traditionally said to have belonged to St. Hedwig, who died in 1243. These glasses bear as their main motifs variations of lion-like animals, griffins or eagles, and often a "Tree-of-Life," and have frequently been attributed to an Egyptian source because of the kinship of these motifs to some on rock crystal vessels from that area. Evidence uncovered in recent archaeological excavations in Novogrudok in southern Russia now points to this area as another possible source of origin of these outstanding glasses, which appear in a number of cases to have been used in the Middle Ages as reliquaries and were later preserved in cathedral treasuries.

Yet the Roman Empire did not find in the East a place of perpetual peace. Far from it, for warfare in one form or another was hardly ever absent, but it may be supposed to have been conducted on rules admitting more latitude and tolerance than those prevailing in northern and western Europe. In any case, conditions were never so bad as to bring glassmaking to an end nor to discourage the development of the higher branches of craftsmanship.

But everything comes to an end. In 1258 Bagdad was sacked, and in 1260 Damascus gave unconditional surrender to Hulagu Khan. Again, in 1300, Damascus was raided by the Tartars, and finally, in 1402, Tamerlane, in a war of conquest, carried off the glassmakers of Damascus to work for him in his distant capital of Samarkand, and the period was thus closed. But what is one man's loss is often another's gain. The extinction of the craft in the Near East created the opportunity for Venice to develop, and a new era was opened whose influence is with us today.

THE DECLINE OF GLASSMAKING IN THE WEST

While a civilization centered in Byzantium existed in the East where the arts flourished, not least that of glass, the position in the West was far otherwise. There, from the fifth century until the thirteenth, glassmaking deteriorated both in quality and accomplishment. Even so, the period is not entirely blank or without interest, for during that time a few new types evolved which were distinct and were, indeed, possible in no other place and at no other time. It is not a period likely to be represented in any small or modest collection, however, chiefly because worthwhile glass was produced in small quantities then. This lack of material has been further diminished by the change in burial customs that came with the acceptance of the Christian faith. The Church in those early days discouraged, or perhaps forbade, the pagan practice of burying coins and utensils with the dead, so that, deprived of the safety of the tomb, much glass must have been destroyed by the havoc of historical events or even by the little accidents which, sooner or later, overtake the best-regulated families.

There is evidence that ordinary utility ware continued to be made, such as palm-cups—that is, cups without handles that were held between the palms of the hands—jugs, and simple household utensils; but the exercise of the craft on the higher artistic levels was restricted and all but lost. But it was not a lost art in the sense that its processes were forgotten, for several medieval writers give recipes and describe methods of manufacture that belong to the Roman period, but which were not necessarily being practiced then. These quaint documents are composed of passages taken from Pliny to which were grafted the formulae of alchemy, which was the chemical science of those days. When one deducts ingredients like fat worms or blood drawn from a fasting goat and other predilections of the magical, what is left has been supplied by Pliny, and from that it might be inferred that these writers were dealing with an art of the past and not with something that was alive in their own day.

Among them, however, is a more reliable authority. Theophilus, who lived in Helmershausen, Westphalia, during the eleventh century, gave a valuable contribution when he wrote his *Schedula diversarum artium*. In a section of that work dealing with glass, Theophilus is closer to reality than his contemporaries, and, for the most part, he describes the activities of the craft as it existed then.

In these accounts the mixture of superstition and science appears to the modern man as childish and ludicrous, but, at bottom, they really indicate an attitude of mind common enough today. The sentiment behind this love of magic sprang from man's everlasting desire to get something for nothing, and what could be more thoroughly modern? Nemesis, one feels, is the proper thing for the other fellow, but is a goddess who will never bring one's self to account. Therefore do we go on burning oceans of petroleum, hacking down forests, hastening, for all we are worth, the process of soil erosion, living in fact on capital without a thought for settling day. In the twentieth century something for nothing is still the ideal, but pursued so wholeheartedly, with such an imposing display of technology and know-howness, applied publicly by political manipulation, privately through the football pools.

Compared to our monstrous belief, how petty are the aspirations of our medieval forefathers. They, modest souls, asked for nothing more than the gift to transmute a lump of scrap lead into an ingot of mere gold. How foolish it seems in their case, how natural and right in ours. In glass this idiotic hankering took the form of changing sand into precious stones; not to make glass *like* a precious stone, but to make glass that *was* a precious stone. And the curious thing is, they believed the miracle had been achieved. They were sure they had it.

There are cups and tables in the treasuries of various European churches which were believed to have been cut from sapphires and emeralds, and slabs of green glass such as "Charlemagne's Emerald" and "King Solomon's Table" were held as rare and very precious things. The most famous of these is a glass bowl of an emerald color now in the Cathedral of S. Lorenzo at Genoa, known as the *Sacro Catino*. This has been variously regarded as a gift from Solomon to the Queen of Sheba, the bowl in which Salome carried the head of John the Baptist, and even the Holy Grail. But whatever part in religious history may now be assigned to it, as a vessel it is generally accepted as being made of Alexandrian glass of the Roman period.

Glassmaking in the Seine and Rhineland areas during the decline of Rome was in the hands of Syrians, a Semitic race gifted artistically and having a realistic commercial sense well able to create and control markets to their advantage. They were also adaptable by nature and able not only to interpret the needs of their patrons, but to conform easily to the customs of the people among whom they had chosen to live.

The withdrawal of Roman troops no doubt made life difficult for them, and the constant invasions and migrations of the northern pagans must have interrupted the natural flow of commerce and even interfered with the exercise of the craft itself, but, nevertheless, as long as there was a market and something to be gained, they held on with the tenacity characteristic of their race.

But things were to go from bad to worse. In the havoc that followed the breaking up of Charlemagne's empire, the transport of goods became impossible. The Roman road system was at an end, and Roman convoys to protect the sea routes had long since ceased and with them the markets of Britain and Scandinavia, so that trade was finished and even Syrian astuteness was unable to make a market. When that happened, the best of the glassmakers gave up the situation as hopeless and migrated to Altare, near Genoa. This took place in the ninth century. Those who were left were not craftsmen of the first rank, and with them remained native workmen who had taken to the trade. But without the stimulus of enterprise or the inspiration of creative genius, and with markets restricted to a locality, the craft lost vitality and could not rise above the making of commonplace articles in *verre de fougère*.

Verre de fougère was a glass natural to the country. The soda used in making this glass was obtained from the ash of bracken. A *verre de fougère* tradition was gradually built up which produced its best artistic work in the fifth and sixth centuries. By the fourteenth century the production of utility glass was by no means inconsiderable.

In the Rhineland a *Waldglas* tradition was developing simultaneously. The alkali used in making this glass may have been taken from bracken, although it is quite likely that it was supplied from the ash of beechwood. Usually it is held that the alkali used in *verre de fougère* came from bracken and that used in *Waldglas* from beechwood. In any case the results were very similar. Both belonged to the forest.

It is sometimes said that *Waldglas* is a primitive glass and that its green color was the result of the materials used then by the glassmakers who lacked the knowledge and skill to change it. This view I think mistaken, because clear glass was being made for windows at that time. There was nothing to hinder glassmakers from using clear glass for vessels, therefore, if they had wanted to do so; but the fashion and taste of the times demanded not only color, but a particular color. And how appropriate that color happened to be to a people who lived in forests! The soft liquid green of *Waldglas* is the green we see through the sunlit leaves of a tree in early summer. It is true that some *Waldglas* is crude and badly fused, but the best examples can hardly be surpassed for texture or for the natural beauty of its rich, living green.

THE CONE BEAKER

In England it is unlikely that glass was made after the Romans had left the country, and it was not until the thirteenth century that the industry was established in the Weald by Laurence *Vitrearius*. That is not to say that glass was not used in England. It seems, indeed, to have been imported from the Continent, or possibly brought by the Saxons and other invaders as part of their more highly esteemed possessions. The graves of Saxons have yielded some glass as good as any of the period, although the bulk of it is rather below the standard of attainment of the glass found in Germany. That more glass exists in England, hidden in un-

Cone beaker found in Northern France.
[*Victoria and Albert Museum photograph. Crown Copyright*]

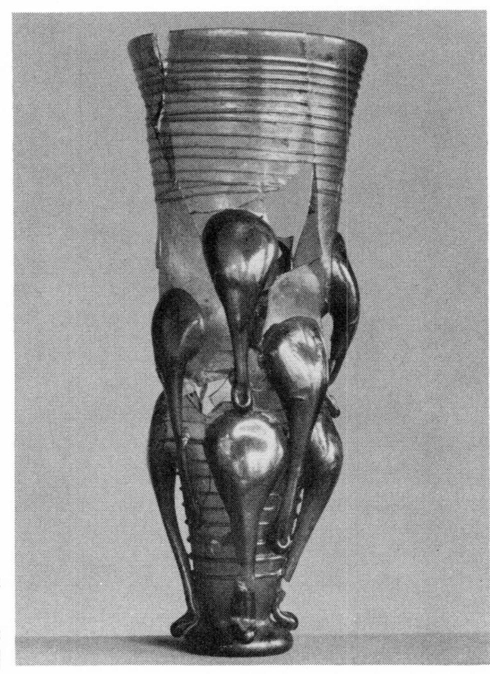

This claw beaker was found at Ashford, Kent.
[*Victoria and Albert Museum photograph. Crown Copyright*]

discovered graves, is certain, and at least some of this will be restored to us as time goes on.

Most of the English glass was made by Syrians working in the Seine or Rhineland areas, but it shows a change of feeling on the part of its creators. In it Eastern shapes have given place to designs that are thoroughly Teutonic in spirit, and trail decoration is used more lavishly and to greater purpose. In earlier examples the Syrian glassmakers seem to have adapted Eastern ideas to the aesthetic responses of their customers, but later the shapes and decoration are wholeheartedly Northern and express not inaptly a kind of splendid, barbaric spirit.

Thus we can see a gradual change asserting itself in which horizontal lines are exchanged for vertical. The first drinking vessels, made in the Roman period, are spherical and sedentary, or made to sit safely on a table. Through various stages the vessels lose bulge, the sides become straight and incline in towards a narrower base like a modern tumbler. Later they become higher, and with height acquire the slim proportions which is one of their main attractions. Finally, the foot of the vessel on which it rests is taken away, and we have the unstable glass known as the cone beaker (*Plate 20*).

Some experts maintain that this lack of a foot is an indication of a decline in skill, that the glassmakers, in fact, did not give their cone beakers feet because they were unable to do so. Yet the best specimens of cone beakers must have demanded a high degree of skill, and it is hardly likely that the men possessing such skill were unable to complete the work by the addition of another comparatively simple operation had they cared to do so.

W. A. Thorpe, in his *English Glass,* holds the view that the development of the cone beaker was the result of the fashion among the Germans of that time. Very probably he is right, and certainly it would be difficult to find a better explanation.

Cone beakers were made for aristocrats, and the quality at that time were hunting and fighting men who needed relaxation at the end of strenuous day's slaughter. The tired hero did not drink sitting at a table, but stretched his weary limbs upon a couch. A servant at his elbow handed him a beaker full of mead, or whatever the popular tipple might be. Such a full-blooded, hearty fellow would not sip his mead or even drink it. He would quaff, and so the vessel would be drained at a single gulp, the empty beaker then exchanged for a full one and the operation repeated, until the warrior rolled off the couch and fell into a gentle doze among the rushes. It was a spacious age!

And when one considers the shape of a cone beaker, one is inclined to ask, was this not a rather refined version of the cruder drinking horn used by the previous generation? Very likely it was, and in making cone beakers the glassmakers were following the sound commercial rule of giving the customer what he wants.

THE CLAW BEAKER

In the East the glassmaker achieved his artistic effects through shape, in the way the vessel was blown, and he usually exercised restraint in applying decoration by the use of trails and other manipulation of the piece during its plastic state. It was the glassmakers of the North who developed trail decoration into a style and gave to this form something of their own.

Trails were applied in different patterns. In some cases, concentric rings or regularly spaced spirals were achieved by revolving the piece on the end of the pipe while a thread was trailed onto it from a gob of hot glass held by an assistant. Other designs, such as vertical loopings or arches, wishbone trails (*Plate 12e*) and snake threads for which Cologne glasshouses are renowned, were applied free hand, with the aid of an assistant. In some cases the trail might be applied before the vessel was completely blown. After the trail had united with the glass of the vessel, blowing was continued, and when the operation was finished the trail stood in low relief and had a tapered effect.

The change from exotic Eastern forms to designs indigenous to the country was gradual, and the development in the use of trails began in Roman times and continued till the fifth and sixth centuries. By that time the designs of the glassmakers in the Seine and Rhineland areas had reached a style distinctly their own. Latterly, drinking vessels were their most outstanding products. That these were prized by their owners is beyond question. Many were brought to England by Jutes, Saxons and other invaders, and that they were esteemed precious is revealed by the tombs that are constantly being discovered in modern times. It was not the commonplace glass that was buried with the Saxon or his wife, but their most treasured pieces.

These drinking vessels are of two kinds: unstable cone beakers, which have already been discussed, and sedentary claw beakers. Claw beakers as a rule (*Plate 20*) are amber colored, or light or dark green. Possibly the claw began as a handle like a certain type of Syrian beaker that has two small handles, as those on a teacup, placed just beneath the rim of the vessel, and possibly the Northern glassworkers made a handle in the shape of a claw. Then a love of decoration supplanted mere usefulness, so that the beaker was at last covered with handles that served no purpose but that of ornament.

But as ornaments these claws seem to emanate from the untamed, barbaric soul. They are fierce and grotesque, like an organic growth, gnarled like the branch of a tree, but a tree seen in a nightmare. To the Germans they seem like elephants' trunks, for their name for them is *Rüsselbecher*; but whether we call them claws or trunks, it is a decoration with more than a hint of the terror that lies hidden in the secret depths of the forest.

Possibly claw beakers began as a demonstration of the glass-maker's virtuosity, but the design happened to have a mystical quality that appealed to the Teutonic mind. One imagines that they were irresistible to the German of that time, and it is easy to see how they became a popular fashion.

Chapter Four

VENETIAN GLASS AND GLASSMAKING IN MEDIEVAL ENGLAND

THE EMERGENCE OF THE VENETIAN GLASSMAKING INDUSTRY

DURING the Renaissance Venice became a universal provider of fine glass, and the supremacy of Venetian workmen throughout the whole period exerted a powerful influence in the Netherlands, France, Germany, England, Spain, and Asia. Tamerlane, in the beginning of the fifteenth century, had extirpated glassmaking in the Near East with a thoroughness of which even a modern dictator would not be ashamed, thereby giving Venice an opportunity of markets none were able to share or dispute, for none had craftsmen capable of the high accomplishment, or inspired with the impulse of the generous, creative spirit that was the glory of this proud republic.

By the thirteenth century Venice had won a reputation for artistic glass which suggests that glassmaking had been in existence there for some time. There are no records of glassmaking before then, however, and the story begins when the craft is already established. In the following century a fair quantity of glass was being exported to different parts of Europe, and certainly by the fifteenth century the Venetians had discovered the use of manganese for making clear glass. In the Roman periods clear glass was never very popular, and it may be that a taste for it was only acquired slowly during the Renaissance. Certainly the fame of Venice, in its earlier years, rested on its colored glass of which its craftsmen had a thorough mastery. The clear glass they made, however, was easily worked, and this condition, exploited to the full by a superb craftsmanship, resulted in elaborate and fine forms that were irresistible, and a new fashion in clear glass was begun.

This glass, which was given the name *cristallo*, was only relatively clear and, when judged by standards of clearness alone, falls short of glass made at a later period in England and Germany. It has, however, a beauty and charm distinctly its own. Usually *cristallo* has a tinge of brown or yellow or black of a smoky, misty quality that is most attractive, and perhaps it was this quality that brought about the blowing of extremely thin glass, for the smoky tinge is most noticeable in thick glass and hardly apparent at all in very thin glass. The silica used for making *cristallo* was obtained from grinding a quartz type of pebble taken from the river Ticino, and the soda was obtained from the ash of seaweed.

By the thirteenth century glassmaking in Venice had become of considerable importance to the economy of the Republic, which was naturally determined to keep such a lucrative industry to itself if it could do so. Through a powerful guild organization, edicts were passed and remained in force for several centuries, regulating the manufacture of glass in the public interest. Craftsmen were not allowed to leave the glassmaking center, or, at any rate, they could only leave under very heavy penalties, and the export of glassmaking apparatus and cullet (the name given by glassmakers to their scrap) was forbidden. These laws were enforced with vigor and thoroughness, but were not wholly effective apparently, for Venetian glassmakers found their way to the Netherlands, Germany, France, Spain, and England, there to set up glasshouses and exercise their craft. Indeed, as early as the thirteenth century, recalcitrant Venetians had established themselves in Bologna, Ferrara, and other Italian towns in defiance of all threats and penalties.

Another regulation passed in the thirteenth century had moved all the bigger glasshouses to the nearby island of Murano because of the number of fires caused by glassmakers' furnaces. None but lesser glasshouses, making beads and small objects, were allowed to remain in Venice itself, and these were only tolerated on condition that they were built at least fifteen paces from the nearest dwelling house.

We have seen how the Syrian glassmakers of northern Gaul migrated to Altare, near Genoa, after the disruption of Charlemagne's empire. A glassmaking industry developed there and was to become a serious rival for the supremacy held by Venice. Altare, too, had a powerful guild, but this subscribed to commercial doctrines fundamentally opposed to those ruling at Venice. The Altarists were imbued with a missionary spirit that aimed at spreading the craft throughout Europe, and glassmakers were encouraged to set up business in other towns and countries; so that, while the Venetians were kept at home, Altarists were at liberty to roam wherever their fancy, or expectation of gain, might lead.

But to say that Venetians were kept at home is only to state the Venetian aim. Like other civic aims, the subversive activities of a minority in the community always stood in the way of perfect attainment, so that in practice even the threat of severe penalties was unable to curb the restless, independent spirit for which glassmakers were notorious. At any rate, Venetians found their way to every glassmaking center in Europe.

In the sixteenth and seventeenth centuries contemporary writers refer to a *façon d'Altare* and a *façon de Venise*, but today it is hardly possible to tell the one from the other. For that matter it is often impossible to tell whether a particular piece of Venetian glass was actually made in Venice at all. The possibility that it was made in England, or the Netherlands, or some other country, by a wandering Venetian or Altarist is ever present.

VENETIAN INNOVATIONS

Very little is known about the early history of glassmaking in Venice. Though documentary evidence indicates a highly productive glass community as early as the twelfth century, no actual glass vessels known to us can be accurately dated before the second half of the fifteenth century. These early vessels of deep red, blue, or green glass were heavily enameled and gilded, undoubtedly a result of Islamic influence.

But in the creative upsurge of the Renaissance new types of glass were to appear which widened the scope for artistic expression and held the promise of exciting possibilities. A period of great and heartening vitality was opening. An unusual glass developed by the Venetians was a multi-colored, marbleized appearing one, often classified under the German term *Schmelzglas*. Such glass often resembles agate, onyx, or chalcedony, and is excellent of its kind.

At a later date came aventurine glass, the invention of which has been attributed to the Miotti family. Aventurine glass is usually brown and opaque, and is spangled over its surface with small particles of metal. It has been said that the name is derived from the Italian, *aventura*, because of the accidental discovery of this glass.

Another Venetian innovation was the creation of ice-glass (*Plate 21*). This glass had a rough, pitted surface and a frosted appearance so that its name is not only apt but obvious. It was made by plunging heated glass into cold water, withdrawing it instantly and reheating. The use of milk-white glass also came in during the latter part of the fifteenth century. This was simply the opaque-white glass used for canes in the making of *latticinio*, and its resemblance to porcelain lent it to a porcelain treatment. Vases in milk-white were decorated by painted gilt scrolls and figures. In the eighteenth century decoration took the form of painted scenes or of pictures dealing with amatory topics in the sophisticated and airy manner of the times. Specimens of sixteenth-century milk-white are rare, but a very good round vase on a foot, decorated with gilt scrolls and mermaids, is to be seen in the British Museum, belonging to what used to be the Azeglio collection. It was not until the eighteenth century that milk-white reached its greatest popularity.

But the greatest contribution to the art made by the Venetians was *cristallo*, which has already been discussed. In its plastic state this glass was easily worked and it became the medium for an artistic expression that was imaginative, delicate, and mercurial (*Plates 22 and 23*). Its importance as a material that lent itself to glass forms cannot be overemphasized. With *cristallo*, glassmakers began to make shapes that belonged to glass and were not imitations of metalwork or some other thing. The tutelage that had lasted throughout so many centuries was now at an end and glass had at last come into its own.

The chief advantage of this new, ductile glass was to enable the glassworker to perform feats that were impossible in a less complaisant metal, so that he could imprint subtleties of feeling

Plate 21 VENETIAN GLASS
This specimen of ice glass is in the Venetian manner although it may not have been made in Murano. It belongs to the sixteenth century.
[*Victoria and Albert Museum photograph. Crown Copyright*]

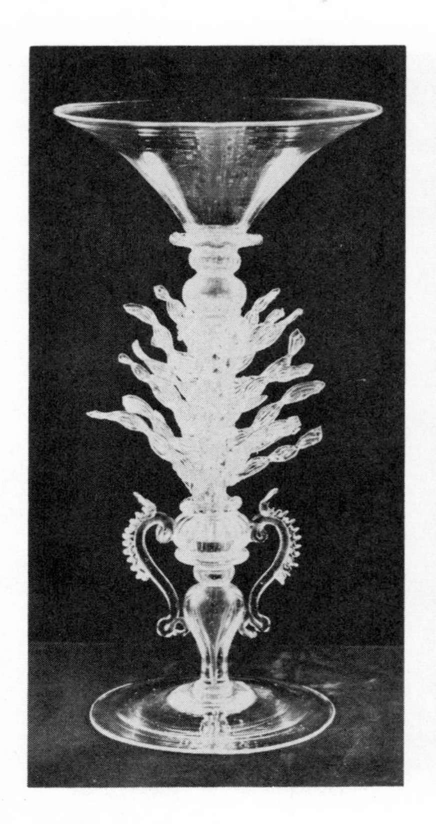

Plate 22 VENETIAN GLASS

These seventeenth-century glasses in the baroque manner demonstrate the Italian temperament when an imaginative worker lets himself go. Their preservation is a tribute to the sobriety of former owners.

[*Victoria and Albert Museum photograph. Crown Copyright*]

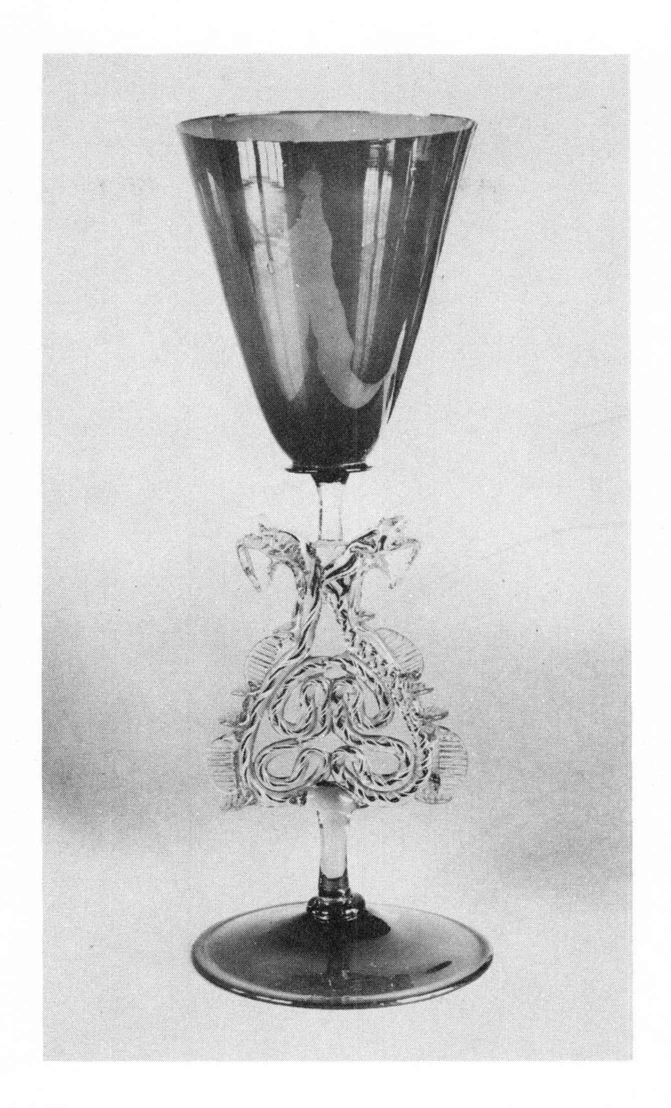

Plate 23 FAÇON DE VENISE GOBLET
This purple goblet has been preserved by the Halkett family of Pitfirrane. According to tradition, James VI drank his stirrup cup from it when leaving Dunfermline to take up his new throne in London.

[*National Museum of Antiquities of Scotland, Edinburgh*]

This exquisite plate illustrates the delicate results obtained in *latticinio*.
[*Victoria and Albert Museum photograph. Crown Copyright.*]

Venetian enameled glass, late fifteenth century.
[*Victoria and Albert Museum photograph. Crown Copyright*]

hitherto lost in the dour qualities of stiffer glass. At first, in the sixteenth century, forms were simple and graceful, but this gave place to an age of baroque extravagance and a bewildering variety of shapes and decoration. In the making of elaborate stems, flared bowls, molded fluting, masque knops, and all kinds of applied decoration the Venetians let themselves go with zest, and their imaginative gifts were often expressed through whimsical and fantastic forms, created, one supposes, in sheer joy and high spirits.

VENETIAN TECHNIQUES

During the late fifteenth century enameling on both colored and colorless glasses became one of the most successful decorative mediums used by Venetian craftsmen. Numerous fine examples have survived bearing allegorical and genre scenes, portraits, and other symbols. Imitations of this work were made in the nineteenth century, but these are not such as to be easily mistaken for genuine specimens.

When *cristallo* came into fashion enameled glass lost popularity. Enamel was not suited to clear glass, although it was sometimes used in a restrained way. Pictures disappeared, and decoration might be in the form of a simple band of colored beads or the shield of arms of some noble owner (*Plate 24*). Armorial glasses were the thing for a while, but the fashion seems to have died out before the close of the sixteenth century.

Diamond-point engraving was another treatment used on clear glass by the Venetians, but this did not have the appeal, nor, indeed, reach the same level of accomplishment, as the engraving done in the Netherlands at a later period.

A far more important artistic development was that of *latticinio*, which, when applied to vases, bowls, or other vessels, gave the effects of fine lace. Such pieces were made by arranging a series of opaque white canes around the sides of a vertically ribbed mold, picking them up on a gather of colorless glass at the end of a blowpipe, re-heating and marvering this, then (sometimes gathering more colorless glass over it) blowing and tooling this into the desired shape. Many *latticinio* designs were possible by arranging the canes in different sequences (*Plate 25, right*).

One more complicated form of *latticinio* decoration in which tiny air bubbles are trapped between the crossed canes is called *vetro di trina*. It is made by first gathering a series of canes arranged in a vertically ribbed mold on the exterior of a parison of glass, which is then twisted to produce a swirled design. This gather, with the swirled canes projecting slightly above its surface, is then inserted again into the mold containing another series of canes which adhere to the surface and thus form a pattern of small diamonds. The whole is then expanded into a thin cup of glass which entraps the air within each diamond. An excellent example of this technique is in the Corning Museum of Glass (*Plate 25, left*).

Latticinio continued in fashion from the sixteenth to the eighteenth century and was a technique practiced in most of the important European glassmaking centers. A good piece, therefore, may be called Venetian, but there is no certainty that it was actually made in Murano, and it would be more accurate to term such pieces *façon de Venise*—in the Venetian style.

With such a surge of creative genius, producing radical changes in technology and technique, giving a new conception of glass, and opening new fields of artistic expression, it is little wonder that Venice dominated the scene. Her influence on France, Spain, the Low Countries, Germany, England, and Scandinavia was overwhelming. Eagerly these countries adopted the Venetian manner, gladly they gave shelter and encouragement to those bands of Venetian workmen who, suffering banishment from their native country for the sake of their art and personal gain, had crossed the frontiers to live among them.

But although Venetian glassmakers had set a fashion in the countries where they had settled, foreign tastes and customs gradually produced changes in these craftsmen as well, and we find the Venetian manner being adapted to local needs and character. These changes are particularly noticeable in Flemish and English glass, where the Italian love of flourish and Italian delicacy and grace give place to a plain and stately massiveness more in keeping with the sober temperament of the North. The story of the rise of Venice in all its ramifications is by no means easily followed, and it should not be forgotten that the men of Altare contributed much to the revival. Thus Genoa has a right to share the honors with Venice.

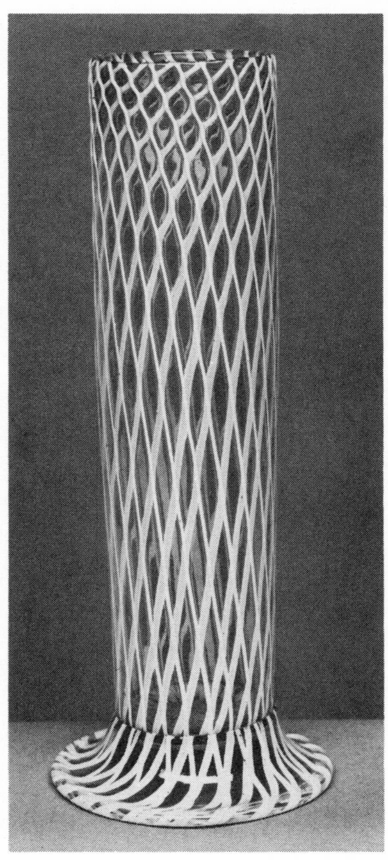

Plate 25 FAÇON DE VENISE

This Venetian style goblet with a whistle, probably made in Germany, is an excellent example of the *vetro di trina* technique. The whistle is marked 1673.

[*The Corning Museum of Glass*]

This *Stangenglas* belongs to the sixteenth century and was probably made in Germany by an Italian craftsman.

[*Victoria and Albert Museum. Crown Copyright*]

THE DEVELOPMENT OF THE ENGLISH GLASS INDUSTRY

European experts do not have a high opinion of English glass. In *Das Glas*, Robert Schmidt, one of the most distinguished as well as one of the most thorough writers on the subject, dismisses English glass in three short pages. But while we are bound to admit that English glass is less plentiful and that it lacks the variety and scope of the more restless and adventurous glass of the Continent, we may rightly claim for it virtues of its own. It excels in a quality that is peculiarly English and that could not have been produced in any other country. For a certain steadfast honesty of purpose, for simplicity and natural grace, English glassmakers have never been surpassed.

The story of English glass begins in the twelfth century with the immigration of foreign glassmakers, and for a long time afterwards the craft remained in foreign hands. After the Romans left Britain, glassmaking diminished, or it may have ceased altogether. The revival during the Middle Ages was on a humble scale, the glass made was a green, somewhat inferior *Waldglas*, and the craft did not rise to the level of artistic expression, nor apparently showed the least ambition to do so. Palm-cups, bottles, and commonplace articles were made in the Roman style, as, indeed, this style continued to be the basis of English design even when better things were possible. In this way the Venetian influence, when it came to England, was the adaptation of an old style to a new, rather than a wholehearted acceptance.

The poor condition of the English craft during that period can be accounted for by the fact that no Syrian glassmakers remained in the country after the Romans had left, so that, even if there had been a demand for better glass and better craftsmanship, it is doubtful if the situation would have been changed in any way. The demand, however, probably did not exist, for the chief, perhaps the only, patron of the arts then was the Church, which forbade the use of glass for making church vessels. It is true that exceptions, such as the Hedwig glasses of Central Europe, were made to this rule, but these exceptions are not numerous and the ban seems to have been universally enforced.

But if the Church prohibited the use of glass vessels for the celebration of Communion, it was the reason for the development of the art of stained-glass windows. Through Church influence and Church encouragement during the Middle Ages this most glorious art reached a pinnacle of achievement that has never been equaled since. In the art of stained glass France was unsurpassed, and the quality of window glass being made there contributed very considerably to this success. Since the ability to make good glass was there, it is strange that an equal skill was not available for making vessels; but so it was, and that branch of the craft in France produced nothing more exciting than commonplace utensils of *verre de fougère* in the traditional Roman style.

French window glass was of two different kinds: broad glass made in Lorraine and crown glass made in Normandy. Crown glass was made by taking a large gather of glass on the end of the blowpipe and blowing it into a somewhat flattened sphere. A pontil was then affixed to this sphere opposite the end of the blowpipe, and the latter cracked off. This left a small hole in the sphere which was gradually enlarged, partly by the aid of a wooden paddle and partly by centrifugal force created by spinning the piece while it was being re-heated. Suddenly, the effects of the centrifugal force caused the remaining semblance of the sphere to flatten into a large circular disk. This was then cracked off the pontil and placed in a lehr or annealing furnace to cool slowly. The raised circular mark, or bullion, left at the center of the disk, or crown of glass, is called today a "bull's-eye," and is highly prized by collectors, but was usually used by glassmakers as cullet. Broad glass was made by blowing a long cylinder of glass from which the ends were removed and which was then slit up its length and flattened into a sheet of glass.

Stained glass was required in England during this time, most of which was imported from France. That glass made in England would have been acceptable had it been available may be inferred from the repeated requests of English churchmen to their brethren in France to send glassmakers to England.

Then, about the year 1226, Laurence *Vitrearius* came from Normandy to establish the glassmaking industry in the Weald. His glasshouse was at Dyer's Cross, Pickhurst, a hamlet near Chiddingfold. He was an able craftsman (E. Barrington Haynes thinks that although he came from Normandy it is possible that he received his training in Altare) and the quality of his products may be judged by the fact that one of his contracts was to supply colored and clear glass for Westminster Abbey.

Although window glass was his main business, there is evidence that he made vessels as well. Laurence *Vitrearius* was followed by his son William, called *le Virrir*. In him the family tradition was in safe hands, and it was largely due to his qualities as a craftsman that Chiddingfold received a Royal Charter in 1300.

There is a Lancashire saying, "clogs to clogs," which describes the rise and fall of family businesses. The grandfather, rising from the status of workman to that of owner and industrialist, discards his workman's clogs for a more refined footwear in keeping with his exalted position. Then the son follows, barely maintaining the position won for him by his sire. And finally the grandson loses all, sinks into obscurity, and assumes once more the workman's clogs. Whether the business founded by Laurence suffered that fate or just died out is unknown, but in fifty years, by 1343, another family from France, the Schurterres, were in control of the Wealden industry.

The Schurterres were associated with John Alemayne, who was a selling agent rather than a worker in glass, but, as W. A. Thorpe points out, he probably had an interest and influence on the kind of glass being produced. It was through his agency that Schurterre supplied glass for St. Stephen's Chapel, Westminster, and St. George's Chapel, Windsor.

Every dog has his day. The Schurterre family were isolated, far removed from the great glassmaking centers of the Continent, and it is perhaps little wonder that they should succumb to the next settler from France, a glassworker called Peytowe, who, equipped with a more progressive knowledge, was soon in the ascendancy. Peytowe came to Chiddingfold in 1435, where he set up a number of glasshouses and gained complete control of the industry, a mastery which was retained until the sixteenth century when the older Wealden tradition was brought to an end by a new phase.

Besides making window glass, the earlier Wealden industry produced glass vessels, but the specimens that survive cannot be placed more particularly than having been made in a period not earlier than 1226 or later than 1550.

A number of vessel fragments were found at Vann which are ascribed to this period. This glass is not of the Roman period and yet does not belong to the later Wealden period when the glass made at that time was of a darker green. The fragments are of vessels having trailed and wrythen decoration. Undoubtedly Laurence *Vitrearius* or his successors, the Schurterres and Peytowes, were the creators of this glass. Other evidence of the making of vessels at this time is documentary. It is recorded that Laurence sold his wares to Henry III, whose son, Edward I, also became a patron of the art, or, at any rate had sufficient interest to buy one or two things.

CARRÉ AND THE LORRAINE WORKERS

Wealden glass began to deteriorate by the middle of the sixteenth century, and in that circumstance Venetian and Lorraine glassworkers saw an opportunity to set up glasshouses in England to capture the markets for themselves. The Venetian adventure was short-lived, and of the eight men who came from Murano to London in 1549 seven returned to Italy within three years, leaving behind them a single survivor, a man called Cassilari. This was followed, in 1565, by an offer from Cornelius de Lannoy to make glass in the manner practiced in the Netherlands, but this promise could hardly be fulfilled, for Cornelius turned out to be an impostor.

The Lorraine workers had a greater success, due largely to the genius of Jean Carré, a man gifted artistically and endowed with strength of mind and force of character. Carré had gained experience in Arras and Antwerp, and when he came to England his intention was to make *cristallo* glass vessels in London and to continue window-glass making in the Weald. This he was able to carry out after prolonged negotiations.

Carré brought several Muranese workers to London and installed them in the Crutched Friars glasshouse where they were joined by a relative of Cassilari, the last of the former contingent. The work prospered, and glassmaking in the Venetian style was continued for over a hundred years.

In the Weald, Carré established four different families for window-glass making. These were Enzell, Tysack, Tittery, and Hoe, all of whom had earned privileges from the King of France. They belonged to *les gentilshommes verriers*. At that time glassmaking in France was considered a gentleman's occupation in which even noblemen might take part without loss of dignity, and the Royal privileges were looked on as a patent of nobility. But in Carré's *gentilshommes* only the worst attributes of nobility, untempered by any of the finer qualities, were apparent. They were proud but lacked good manners, impulsive but without grace, qualities that did not commend them to those with whom they lived.

Carré's dealings with the established glassmakers in the Weald might be described as unscrupulous, but he had the astuteness to maintain a working agreement with others not clever or strong enough to oppose him. But this he was unable to do without causing hidden resentment, and his death was the immediate signal for a revolt by those whom he had overreached and outwitted. His Lorraine workers were the scapegoats, and it was they who suffered for his too able management.

The old-established glassmakers of the Weald joined with the ironworkers, who were indignant at the inroads made by the Lorrainers into the available stock of fuel. This was the pot calling the kettle black, for when it came to cutting down whole forests to supply billets for their smelting furnaces the ironworkers had no equal. Nevertheless, the Lorraine glassworkers used considerable quantities of fuel, and when their glasshouses were closed down there would be all the more wood for melting iron. It was to their advantage, therefore, for the ironworkers to join with the established glassmakers in clearing out those unconscionable destroyers of good trees, the Lorraine glassworkers.

Things were made so hot for the Lorrainers that in two years most of them had left the district. Doubtless it was a cruel and unjust dispensation, but in the end it brought advantages to the country, for glassmaking was established throughout the land, in Buckholt, Hampshire, in Gloucestershire, in Blore Park near Eccleshall, in Stourbridge, in Cheswardine, and in Newcastle-on-Tyne.

All that remains of the Lorraine glass blowers' activities are fragments, but these are sufficient to enable us to assess their achievements. In thin blown glass, with stems that aped the elegance of the Netherlands glass, the Lorrainers are deficient, but in glass blown in a single piece, in tall drinking vessels, they excelled. This was an art of their own, lesser no doubt than the German art that produced the *Spechter*, the *Krautstrunk*, and the *Römer*, but, for all that, excellent of its kind. In work of this kind

W. A. Thorpe gives the Lorrainers a high place when he writes: "If we had the green beakers entire I suspect they would take a place beside Verzelini's 'Venice glasses,' a different but not inferior art." Thus ended the medieval phase of the art in England and as it closed the modern phase was already begun.

Chapter Five

VERZELINI, SIR ROBERT MANSELL, AND GEORGE HAY

GIACOMO VERZELINI

WHEN Carré, in 1568, set out to make *cristallo* at the Crutched Friars works in London, he attempted to do so by employing Lorraine workers. It was an essay doomed to failure from the start, for these men had been trained in the Northern tradition of Gothic stateliness which made it difficult for them to adapt themselves to the classic idiom of the Venetian style, for which, doubtless, they had little feeling and less understanding. This unsuccessful experiment continued for two years and at the end Carré was obliged to bring into the country six Venetian glassmakers of proved ability. In them his ambition was realized, but, alas for human hopes, he did not live to see the fulfillment of his dreams. Carré died in 1572, less than a year after the arrival of that band of Venetian workers on which so much depended.

Acting as manager of this group was Giacomo Verzelini, who took Carré's place when he died and carried the work to a triumphant fulfillment. Verzelini is one of the great figures of English glassmaking and may be counted the founder of the modern phase of the art. He was a wise man and a superb craftsman with a sensitive feeling for design, he was upright in all his dealings, enjoyed a happy family life, earned the genuine respect of all who worked with him, and was a thoroughly lovable soul who came to be known as "Mr. Jacob."

Verzelini was born in Venice in 1522. When he had mastered

his craft he emigrated to Antwerp, where he prospered and married a lady of good family. He was forty-nine when he and his wife came to London, trailing behind them a string of lusty young children. Then, when Carré died, he took over the concern appointing Cassilari[1] as his manager.

His is a success story, the kind of story that begins with a friendless man standing alone to face terrible odds, and ends with a fortune and a name enshrined in the Roll of Fame. Early in his career he met with strenuous opposition from a number of London merchants who were importing glass from Venice and elsewhere, and the position was made the more difficult for him by the fact that he was not a naturalized subject and had, therefore, no standing in the community. The relationship between him and the merchants deteriorated, going from bad to worse, until the merchants, exasperated by Verzelini's success, vindictively set fire to his premises in an attempt to ruin and utterly destroy him and as a lesson to other presumptuous upstarts.

This dastardly deed was done on a Sunday when Verzelini and his family were innocently in church worshipping God. It was a tremendous blaze, made the more terrible by the huge stock of fuel stored in the building (Holinshed says there were about forty thousand billets of wood), and when it had burnt itself out nothing but the charred walls remained.

It is true that the cause of the fire was never explained and that, in the lack of evidence, it would be unjust to blame Verzelini's trade opponents; but whoever had doubts, Verzelini had none. He immediately applied to the Privy Council for protection and asked for a Royal privilege giving him a monopoly in glassmaking. The request was vigorously opposed by his enemies, who tried every means in their power to subvert the plea—but in vain; Verzelini's cause prevailed and, in 1575, Queen Elizabeth granted a license to Giacomo Verzelini "to make drinking glasses in the manner of Murano, on the undertaking that he bring up in the said Art and Knowledge our natural subjects."

The terms of the license were so honorably executed by Verzelini that no fewer than fifteen glasshouses were established in London shortly afterwards. This famous monopoly was given Verzelini for twenty-one years. Furthermore, the importation of

[1] See page 46.

glasses made in Venice was prohibited, although the prohibition does not appear to have been rigorously enforced.

In granting the license Queen Elizabeth was, no doubt, actuated by a desire for the country's good and wished to see a glass industry of the first rank established in England, but it says much for Verzelini's character and reputation and the justice of his cause that he was able to overcome the forces of vested interest and jobbery ranged against him. A year later he became a naturalized subject. The Crutched Friars glasshouse was rebuilt and another opened in Broad Street. And the rest is a story of uninterrupted prosperity.

Verzelini's products soon won him a high reputation, he had the patronage of the nobility, and many of his old enemies, the merchants, as soon as they smelled a chance of profit, became his best customers. It was a success built by talent and integrity, untainted by greed or ruthlessness, and Mr. Jacob, as Verzelini came to be called, earned the respect of his neighbors by his simple dignity. He was a man in whom the growing colony of Muranese workers found a good master and loyal friend. His fortune was made and, at seventy, Verzelini retired to his country house, Valons, at Downe, where he lived for another fourteen years, a wealthy man and venerable patriarch.

During the twenty working years of his life in London, Verzelini must have produced a vast quantity of glass and it is to be regretted that so little of it can be identified today. Doubtless a good deal of it still exists but has become lost among the glasses classified as Venetian, for it is not always possible, indeed it is rarely so, to distinguish Venetian glass made in Venice from Venetian glass made elsewhere by Venetian workers in the Venetian manner.

There are nine glasses known that are attributed to Verzelini. All but one of these bear diamond point engraving attributed to Anthony de Lysle, later known as Lisley, an engraver who came from France and worked on his own account in London. One of these glasses is decorated entirely with gilding; some of the others still bear some traces of such decoration, in addition to the diamond point engraving (*Frontispiece*). Examples of Verzelini's work may be seen in the Victoria and Albert Museum, the British Museum, and in the Corning Museum of Glass.

Verzelini's business was taken over by Sir Jerome Bowes, who received a monopoly for twelve years when Verzelini's license expired. He was granted a second monopoly later. Sir Jerome was an old soldier who had gone into glassmaking in order to turn an honest penny. His talents, however, were directed to the kind of intrigue needed to secure monopolies, and his interest in glassmaking was mainly commercial, but, for all that he was no craftsman, he did seem to maintain Verzelini's tradition for a while. For this satisfactory state of affairs he had his workmen to thank, but he does not seem to have been noticeably grateful. He was a violent man with an ungovernable temper, always kicking one or other of his workmen out of the door and sending to Antwerp for others. And when, at the end of the day, he made nothing by his commercial enterprise, no one need pretend to be sorry.

At this time the Government became concerned at the depredations made to the country's oak forests, which were fast being cut down to supply the furnaces of glassworkers with fuel. At last, in 1615, it was found necessary to make the *Royal Proclamation Touching Glass*, which prohibited the use of wood for fuel. This edict made great changes, because, up to this time, coal had been found unsuited for glassmaking. It was difficult to prevent specks of soot, ash, or sulphurous fumes from mixing with the metal and contaminating it, but this difficulty was removed by the timely invention of Thomas Percivall, who discovered a way to use coal without its former disadvantages. Among those who adopted Percivall's technique were Sir Edward Zouche and Company, who had been granted a patent after the expiry of Sir Jerome Bowes's first monopoly.

SIR ROBERT MANSELL

The shape of the glassmaking industry came to be greatly influenced by the system of monopolies beloved of the Stuarts. In our day, words like monopoly and cartel have a sinister and reprehensible meaning, but it should be remembered that, in the seventeenth century, monopolies were considered a natural and sound commercial practice, the accepted thing not only in England but throughout the civilized world. It was a phase in our political development, perhaps a necessary one, without which glassmaking might not have survived.

The system brought into prominence Sir Robert Mansell, a

man gifted with the skill for Court intrigues and one destined to become outstanding in the history of English glass. But although Sir Robert's greatness is never disputed, it is often implied that there is something dubious about it, or that it is something to which he had no just title. He was no artist, it is true; he was not even the kind of man who could have acquired the craftsman's sleight-of-hand or taken a delight in manual accomplishment, and it is doubtful if he had any feeling for the art at all. His talents were all the other way, and when he took up glassmaking he was frankly out to make money. Profit being his main interest, he was not concerned with the quality of material or workmanship as such, but only with quality in relation to cost, which, in the end, means bringing down quality to price and never raising price to quality.

To the craftsmen who worked for him he was, at the best, a thorn in the flesh, a man without feeling, incapable of recognizing merit when he saw it, and one whose money-grubbing was quickly reducing the art to the level of a mere trade, but whose existence was, in some unaccountable way, indispensable, and who, therefore, had to be endured.

Certainly his outlook was incompatible with the best traditions of the art and, had it been allowed to persist for too long, it must have killed any vital quality and made further progress impossible. Yet it happened that Sir Robert Mansell had just the qualities that were needed to give direction to the craft at that time. Throughout the country glassmaking then was disjointed and without aim. Craftsmen were isolated, there was little change of ideas or possibility of that specialization wherein each district may give the kind of services for which it is naturally fitted.

It was in the field of organization and finance that Sir Robert gave such an important contribution to glassmaking. It was he who created an industry by co-ordinating isolated units, who gave the industry direction and established it for all time by making it a factor of considerable importance to the economy of the realm.

This financial genius, whose ideas were so far in advance of his times, was born in Morgan, Glamorganshire, in 1573. He made seafaring his career and served in the Navy with distinction, rising to the rank of admiral and being given command of the Fleet of the Narrow Seas. About 1608 he became Treasurer of the

Navy, a lucrative post he was well able to fill and which, one supposes, he worked to his own advantage, as every good treasurer was expected to do in those days.

He was still attached to the Navy when he joined Sir Edward Zouche and Company, who were making glass in London under letters patent. This new life suited him admirably and soon captured his interest, and demanded so much of his time that he retired from the Navy to devote himself wholeheartedly to business. In 1620, however, he was recalled to his country's service and given command of an expedition being sent against the pirates of Algiers. The period of his absence hardly lasted a year, and during this time his affairs were managed by his wife, a woman possessed of great drive and real executive ability, but cursed, unfortunately, with a propensity for interfering in the work of craftsmen about which she knew nothing. There can be no doubt that she was a fit mate for such a man, but, alas, nothing is perfect in this world, and her inconsiderate interference added to Sir Robert's difficulties as time went on.

When he returned from the Algerian expedition, Sir Robert contrived to clear all his partners from the management of Sir Edward Zouche and Company, so that he became sole owner of the concern and could now organize the industry according to his own notions. At the same time he received a grant of letters patent giving him the virtual monopoly of glassmaking in England and Wales. This he wanted to extend to include Scotland, but he was unable to do so.

His position at Court and the fact that he stood high in the King's favor might have realized his ambition to take over the Scottish industry had it not been for the opposition of George Hay, the owner of a glasshouse near Wemyss, in Fifeshire. George Hay, too, had Court influence and was able to strike a bargain with that astute monarch, James I, which carried the right for Hay to sell his products in England and Wales.

Nevertheless, Sir Robert Mansell had control in England and Wales and was able either to crush small glassmakers out of business or to buy such concerns over, until he owned glasshouses in every part of the country from Newcastle to London. In the end he was able to buy the Scottish glassworks as well and so realize his ambition to have complete mastery of the industry throughout the United Kingdom.

He was not a practical glassmaker and, therefore, was entirely dependent on his workmen. An arrangement of this kind requires tact on both sides if it is to work smoothly, but as it never entered his head to treat his "servants" with anything more conciliatory than the manners of the quarter-deck, and as his workmen were proud and touchy artisans, madly jealous of their independence, Sir Robert had never his troubles to seek.

CONTEMPORARY CRITICISM

Having control of the entire industry in England and Wales, Sir Robert Mansell made every kind of glass, including mirrors and window glass. His artistic glass was made in the Broad Street glasshouse, where Captain Francis Bacon was appointed manager. For this work it was necessary to employ Venetians or Altarists, for there were no native workers capable of fine craftsmanship.

Naturally Sir Robert being Sir Robert and the Italian workers being Italian, displays of temper and outbursts of passion were commonplace. Usually these storms ended when the Italians packed up their tools and walked out. They hardly cared two straws that they had broken their contracts with Sir Robert Mansell and, untroubled in conscience, they made their way to Scotland to try their luck there with George Hay. The situation was aggravated by Hay's agent in London, Leonardo Michelli, a blackguard who stooped to any means to recruit workmen for the Scottish concern. Sir Robert Mansell, black in the face, was left calling down curses from Heaven on all Italians and their works; then, when he had calmed down sufficiently, he sent to the Netherlands for more Italians and the same situation began over again.

Beyond question the best of Sir Robert Mansell's craftsmen was Antonio Miotti, an artist of Verzelini's stature. Miotti worked for four years in Broad Street, but his stay in London was not very happy. Captain Francis Bacon, the manager, was a soldier, unfitted by temperament and training to wheedle a proud artist or get the best from him. In addition, Lady Mansell kept intermeddling, so that, between them, Miotti had a poor time of it, until at last he threw up his job and returned to the Netherlands.

This continuous changing of staff resulted in glass of unequal quality, and the reports about Mansell's glass vary a good deal.

Unfortunately, our assessment must be based on documentary evidence for the most part, for all that remains of his better class of work are some fragments. When one considers the large quantity of glass that must have been produced, however, it is likely enough that quite a number of unidentified Mansell glass exists today and that these have become mixed with collections of glasses made elsewhere in the Venetian manner and thus are indistinguishable from them.

Of contemporary criticism, the opinion of Inigo Jones cannot be ignored. In his view Mansell's window glass was poor and of unequal thickness. This criticism, however, was made in the early stages of the Mansell period, and better work was doubtless done afterwards when the experience of years had taught its lesson.

Contemporary reports of the drinking glasses differ. Some have said they were good, others that they were bad; but it would not be unreasonable to suppose that both were right, for the quality was almost bound to reflect the emotional tension ruling from time to time. During periods of wrangling the quality would deteriorate, but in periods of comparative calm it would improve. Like the little girl with the curl in the middle of her forehead:

> When it was good it was very, very good,
> But when it was bad it was horrid.

That Mansell's *cristallo* did on occasions reach a high level of artistic merit may be accepted on the testimony of a most unwilling witness. The Venetian Ambassador in London admitted that the glass was good, and he was no friend to Mansell.

At that time the Ambassador was doing everything in his power to persuade immigrant Venetians to return to their own country, and those of his countrymen who defied his directions earned his unconcealed contempt. To him they were traitors giving away secrets that belonged exclusively to Venice, and he was only too glad to point out that these exiles were "low born" and that their work was coarse and much inferior to the glass of Murano. However, after the arrival of Miotti he changed his tune and sent a report home to the effect that: " . . . various subjects of your Serenity, some outlaws who have taken refuge in this Kingdom, where many natives of Murano may now be met, work at making looking glasses or flint glass or teach how to make them. One of them, so I am informed, has given instructions how to make curved flint glass, Murano fashion, another how to make it better, so that there are many English who work admirably, and the crystal attains a beauty not sensibly inferior, but of quite equal quality to that of Murano, which used once to have pre-eminence and was the pride of the world."

The fact that Sir Robert Mansell was not himself a craftsman made these fluctuations in quality inevitable. On the administrative side, however, the man was a genius, whose gifts for organization increased production and lowered prices, thereby extending the use of glass to a wider public. Of "cristall glasses made by me," he says, "these were formerly 16s. per dozen and are now sold for 5s. 6d. per dozen, and the dearest, being extraordinary fashions, for 7s. per dozen."

And so, through a long catalog of his wares he is able to show reduction in the prices, a condition made possible by his management. His keenness for business kept him alert to current fashions and trends, and spurred him to look for new uses for glass that could be profitably exploited. This led him into experimenting with the manufacture of new products, among which was the making of mirrors. This section of the craft, indeed, was introduced into England by him. Another innovation was the making of wine bottles. These, however, were not wine bottles in the sense accepted today, but were rather decanters for carrying wine from the cask to the table. The shapes of these bottles are picturesque and most attractive.

He encouraged, too, a trade in "extraordinary fashions" and "bespoke glass." Extraordinary fashions included glasses with winged stems, figure-of-eight stems, *latticinio* stems and other elaborate work. Bespoke glasses were glasses made to the designs of, or designed specially for, particular customers. These glasses were used for special occasions and celebrations, and took the form of grotesque representations of fish, beasts, birds, and other fantastic shapes. It was fine, delicate glass, not made to endure, and doubtless much of it was smashed during the hilarity of its first appearance on the table.

The control of many different works and the production of so many diverse types were not without worry. No manufacturer of our own day ever grumbled more about labor troubles and mounting costs than did Sir Robert Mansell, but, indeed, he often had good reason to complain. The faults at the root of his continual disagreements with his workers were by no means all on one side, and he suffered much from the rapacity of his Scottish coal suppliers.

There can be little doubt that glassmaking under his direction received an impetus and that he conferred many benefits upon it. He imported barilla and was the first to bring Stourbridge clay into general use for making covered pots necessary for glassmaking by coal. (The pre-eminence of Stourbridge clay, by the way, still exists today.) He developed coal mining at Newcastle and at South Wales, solely for the sake of glassmaking; he paid very high wages to his workmen and, whatever his shortcomings on the artistic side may have been, these were outweighed by his gifts for management, for it was management that was the crying need at that time.

GEORGE HAY

So long as wood was the only fuel possible for glassmaking, Scotland could not become a glassmaking country, for the land was not excessively stocked with timber. When coal came to be used, however, the situation was changed in Scotland's favor, for Scotland had the advantage of coal that was easily worked and was seemingly limitless. After the invention of the covered pot it was not long before Scotland began making glass. The founder of the industry there was George Hay, a man with aristocratic connections and the kind of influence at Court able to secure the monopoly without which no industrial enterprise of any size could be launched.

George Hay was educated at Pont-à-Mousson in France, and it was during his stay there that the idea of setting up a glasshouse in Scotland occurred to him. To do so required deft handling at Court, but this he was well qualified to do both by circumstance and ability. Fortunately, he stood high in the Royal favor and was able to secure his monopoly even against the strenuous opposition of that other favorite and astute courtier, Sir Robert Mansell.

Among other Court appointments, George Hay was a Gentleman of the Bedchamber. He was, too, an adviser to the Prince, later to become the luckless Charles I, and was regarded as a coming man, active in business and upright in character, and "far ben," as the Scots say, with the King. Later, during Charles's reign, he was created Viscount Dupplin and Lord of Kinfauns.

When he became interested in glass he brought to Scotland a number of glassmakers from France and set up a glasshouse in a bay near Wemyss, in Fifeshire, a place associated with Mary Queen of Scots, for it was here that she was secretly married to Lord Darnley. The site was wisely chosen, for supplies of coal, suitable sand and seaweed, for making kelp to supply alkali, were at hand. Furthermore, the finished products could be shipped from the works and carried across the Firth of Forth to Leith and Edinburgh, which was a far safer means of conveyance than the primitive road transport of the times.

His request to make window glass and bottles received the Royal consent and work was begun. At its best the Scottish industry was an extension of the English one, and it did not show any particular national characteristic or contribute anything new. The quality of the glass was never high. We may take Inigo Jones's word for that, for if Inigo Jones thought little of English glass, he thought less of the Scottish product.

A commission set up by the Scottish Parliament to inquire into the glass industry at that time thought the window glass passable but took a poor view of the table glass being produced. It recommended that specimens of English-made wineglasses be shown at Edinburgh Castle as a standard to which Scottish workers might aspire in time.

A state of ruthless competition soon developed between George Hay and Sir Robert Mansell. Sir Robert's attitude towards his workmen, or "servants" as he called them, no doubt partly accounted for the fact they they were constantly leaving his employment, but that they should all go to Scotland was more than coincidence and there is little doubt that Hay's unscrupulous agent in London, Leonardo Michelli, exploited the circumstance. Then, again, Sir Robert depended on shipments of Scottish coal for his Broad Street glasshouse, and the price of this was suddenly raised to a prohibitive figure which brought his work to a standstill. It would be difficult to say whether or not George Hay was responsible for this state of things, but in all likelihood he had a finger in the pie. According to Sir Robert Mansell, he had spent £33,000 bringing his work to perfection, and there is little wonder that he complained so bitterly that the whole enterprise was being overthrown by the embargo.

And so the fight went on. It seemed to Sir Robert Mansell that the only way to rid himself of the ruinous competition was to buy the Scottish works, but George Hay consistently refused to sell. The two rivals met for the first time at the funeral of their royal master. It was not an occasion suited for recrimination or even a quiet business discussion, and the only permissible relief to their feelings must have been a scowl or occasional snort, which these two experienced courtiers would no doubt contrive to pass off as marks of grief.

Then George Hay took ill. Gout laid him low and he was no longer fit for business. He sold his glasshouse to Thomas Robinson, a London merchant, but Thomas, sly dog, turned out to be an agent for Sir Robert Mansell; and so Sir Robert had the last laugh after all. Well, perhaps not, for the Scottish works turned out a failure on which he lost considerably. Sir Robert was in his grave long before the Scottish industry became established on a proper footing.

Chapter Six

THE RESTORATION—DEVELOPMENT IN SCOTLAND

THE RISE OF THE GLASS SELLERS' COMPANY

AMONG Cromwell's many sterling qualities could not be numbered a love of beauty or a feeling for lovely things. At the beginning of his dictatorship this blind spot hardly mattered, for democracy was still rejoicing in its victory over an outworn aristocracy. It had unbelievably arrived into the fulfillment of its highest aims; the Kingdom of Heaven was at hand, and all men were free.

Then gradually the shouting died away and in the mood of sober reflection that followed it was seen that freedom had been bought at a price. The age anticipated Jean-Jacques Rousseau and his *Social Contract*, too aptly demonstrating the doctrine that "men must be forced to be free." Nevertheless, a standing army and an arbitrary rule were distasteful to English instincts, and it is little wonder that no one thought the new freedom a very precious thing. Furthermore, a drab austerity brought with it a longing for a more graceful way of life, and men began to wish for a future that would restore the kindliness of former times.

Business suffered through the imposition of restrictions as did the arts, not least that of glass, for glass had too close an association with church windows and wine, and other abominations detested by the Puritan mind. For all that, glass had become too useful to be dispensed with entirely, and its manufacture was allowed in a limited way. Mansell's monopoly, of course, was no longer valid, and in the period of the Civil War the industry once again reverted to a number of individual craftsmen working independently.

By 1660, bigotry and intolerance had outstayed their welcome, everyone was heartily sick of restrictions and saw in the Restoration a new and enlivening hope. As it turned out, that hope was not betrayed, and when Charles II returned, the happy event was the signal for a march forward into a world of wider horizons. Two years later the Royal Society was formed, science became applied to industry, and the age was one of exploration and exciting discovery.

Glassmaking was caught in the prevailing mood of optimism, and the times brought into prominence two important factors in shaping the future trends of the industry. The first of these was the rise of the Glass Sellers' Company, the other the interest shown in the craft by George Villiers, second Duke of Buckingham.

The Glass Sellers' Company received a renewed charter from Charles II in 1664. Its first charter was given in 1635, although it had been in existence some time before that. In 1637 it was associated with the Glaziers Company, a society that was inaugurated as far back as 1628, when the two combined to protest against the poor quality of Mansell's glass.

During the Restoration period the Glass Sellers' Company had an important influence on the industry both in maintaining a high quality of glass and in the production of good design. This influence lasted over a hundred years, and it was the Glass Sellers' Company that dictated policy by its expert knowledge of what the public wanted most, and how that need was to be satisfied in a way that would be a credit to the craftsman's artistic powers and a compliment to the good taste of the buyer.

The Glass Sellers' Company was importing glass from Murano, but it did not meekly accept the designs the Muranese makers had to offer. Instead, the Company drew designs of their own adapted to English taste and predilection, and the makers then produced the glass accordingly, although it would be truer to say that they tried to do so. A correspondence between two members of the Company, Measey and Greene, with Alessio Morelli of Murano is now preserved in the British Museum. Through this correspondence it is clear that the Glass Sellers' Company knew what its English customers wanted. Morelli, at first, inclined to interpret the designs given him too freely, and the letters begin to give minute directions on how things were to be done.

About four hundred of Greene's full-size drawings still exist to bear testimony to the devoted labor given in the cause of making English design perfect. One of the difficulties of this trade was the loss from breakages during transport, and it is likely that this consideration stimulated the Company to experiment with the production of good glass at home.

The Duke of Buckingham's interest in glassmaking probably arose from one of the prevailing fashions. At that time science was the thing, and glass was one of the industries to which science might be applied with far-reaching results that would add luster to the name of a noble patron. Also, profits were to be made. At any rate the Duke was drawn into the industry, a few months after Charles II had resumed his crown, by a Frenchman, Jean de la Cam, who persuaded him to invest £6,000 in the venture.

The Duke was able to obtain patents, and during the next fourteen years he dominated the industry, not, it must be admitted, by the possession of any skill or knowledge of the subject, or even by the diligence and perseverance shown by his predecessor, Sir Robert Mansell, but by having the sense to pay high wages for good men and by refraining from interfering with those who understood their business. In this way he enlisted the services of outstanding craftsmen like John Billingham, Thomas Powlden, Morton Clifford, and Thomas Tilson.

One could not expect a duke, least of all the Duke of Buckingham, to turn out to business every morning with the regularity of a city clerk. After all, many graver and gayer matters demanded his attention, and no one will be surprised to be told that he was often absent, or, perhaps it would be truer to say, he was seldom there. That was not a bad thing. His presence in a glasshouse must have been upsetting to those employed there. On the other hand, his attendance at Court must have been very helpful, for there would be little difficulty in securing a patent when his name was attached to the application; furthermore, glass became a popular fashion by his patronage, so that the best service he could have rendered to the industry was to stay away. This he seems to have been able to do admirably.

In the Duke's absence decisions had to be made by those left in charge, and because of this circumstance the Glass Sellers'

Company were consulted and given a freedom to direct the trend of business that might not have been possible had the industry been under the personal supervision of the noble owner. The results were good, for the makers were made to work to exacting standards and were kept in touch with the kind of designs that had the widest appeal. But the advantages were by no means on one side, and it may be that this co-operation between the producers and the selling agency led the Company itself to pursue the researches which later resulted in Ravenscroft's discovery of lead glass.

Very few examples of Buckingham glass exist today, or, at any rate, can be identified as such. The "Royal Oak" goblet commemorating the marriage of Charles II and a narrow wineglass known as the "Scudamore Flute" are said to be the work of the Duke's men, but although there is a strong probability that these claims are true there is no absolute certainty.[1]

THE DISCOVERY OF FLINT GLASS

In the correspondence between Greene and Alessio Morelli, Greene had threatened to make glass at home if Murano could not supply glass more in conformity with his specifications. This was no idle threat, and it happened that the new spirit of scientific investigation then on foot made it possible for Greene to carry it out, although, in that age of exploration, it is hardly likely that the Glass Sellers' Company could have refrained from initiating its experiments to find a substitute for Venice glass even if that glass had been all that could have been desired.

Science was then opening up new possibilities for industry, and glassmaking was one of the first industries to make use of the assistance chemists were able to give it. Dr. Merret had already provided the first textbook on glass to be written in English by translating Neri's *L'Arte Vetraria*, probably at the request of the Glass Sellers' Company, and the attitude of the leaders of the industry was regulated by a spirit of critical investigation.

In 1674 the Glass Sellers' Company built a glasshouse in an isolated position at Henley-on-Thames for the sole purpose of conducting experiments in the manufacture of glass to equal Muranese *cristallo*. These experiments culminated in the discovery

[1] See page 122.

of lead glass, which is England's greatest contribution to the industry. Lead glass, therefore, was not the result of accident or of an empiric development, but was something deliberately planned and achieved through scientific investigation.

At that time the Glass Sellers' Company was dissatisfied with Muranese glass and was ready to treat with any English maker able and willing to fulfill their exacting standards. A likely man seemed to be George Ravenscroft who, in 1673, had been granted a patent for seven years for making "a particular sort of crystalline glass resembling rock crystal," and the Company came to terms with him. Ravenscroft was not a craftsman. He was a technologist, one of the men of that new age who had taken to chemistry, and he is the first glassmaker to have seriously directed scientific techniques to the craft and to have specialized in the making of the metal alone, leaving design and workmanship to others. His father was a prosperous shipowner, he had the advantages of money and a good education, and probably took an interest in glassmaking because of his father's business connections in Venice, where, indeed, he spent a short time acting as his father's agent.

An agreement between Ravenscroft and the Glass Sellers' Company was made in April 1674 whereby Ravenscroft was to supply glass to the Company but was at liberty to sell his surplus production on his own account. Some months later a second agreement was signed giving Ravenscroft permission to build another glasshouse at Henley-on-Thames. This new works was inconveniently situated, but it had the great advantage of privacy so that it was kept for purposes of research while another glasshouse at Savoy, in London, produced such marketable glass as had passed the experimental stages at Henley-on-Thames.

The aim was to produce a crystal glass with the raw material available in England. Hitherto Italian pebbles had supplied the silica for this kind of glass, but English flint was used instead, a circumstance from which is derived the term "flint glass." Not long afterwards it was discovered that sand provided an equally suitable silica, and as sand did not need to be ground and calcined, as was necessary with flint, it came into general use. The name "flint glass," however, continued to be used, as it continues to this day. At the same time Spanish barilla was replaced by potash, and the English glassmakers were thus independent of foreign materials.

The main problem confronting George Ravenscroft at the start of his experiments lay in the fact that flint does not fuse easily. To overcome this fault he increased the quantity of alkali, but, in doing so, upset the balance of the composition of the metal, so that the glass turned out diseased or crizzelled—that is to say, the glass became obscured by a fine network of internal cracks.

If crizzelling were to be eliminated, it was clear that the proportion of alkali must be reduced and some other agent introduced to obtain an easily fused glass. It was then that he mixed red lead with the batch, at first in small quantities but later in much greater proportions. When the technology was properly understood, the proportion of red lead was almost equal to a third of the total weight.

The immediate result was successful, or so it seemed, and glasses made to the new formula were stamped with a seal representing a raven's head to distinguish them from the earlier glasses. Time, however, proved that the new glasses bearing the seal were not what they appeared to be when taken from the lehr, for these, too, began to show signs of crizzelling.

The experiments continued, and although Ravenscroft succeeded in occasionally striking a balance between alkali and silica he was not able to repeat his successes at will. It rested with his successor, Hawley Bishop, to bring the experiments to a successful issue. Ravenscroft died in 1681, and it was not until 1682 that the new flint glass was in full production, so that he did not live to see his methods accepted as established practice, nor to rejoice in having provided a glass through which English taste and feeling were to find such an apt expression.

The new glass was softer and heavier than Venetian *cristallo*: it did not readily lend itself to being blown thin, but, on the other hand, it was more substantial and useful, besides having a beauty and attractiveness distinctly its own. Since it was comparatively soft glass, it was admirable for deep cutting, a characteristic which was to be fully exploited in the second half of the eighteenth century, and later. It had great brilliance and a quality never seen before, which seemed to hold its own inner fire. Indeed, the properties of a good piece of cut lead glass to reflect light nearly approach that of the diamond.

A comparison between cut glass and a diamond is shown by

Arnold Fleming in his *Scottish and Jacobite Glass* as the diamond having a dispersing power of 44 and flint glass of 36. Ordinary rock crystal he places at only 14. It is little wonder, then, that Ravenscroft's new glass very quickly gained popularity, and that before the close of the seventeenth century nearly a hundred glasshouses throughout the country were making this kind of glass.

The discovery of this new glass, which gave England command of the world market, must be attributed to the painstaking researches of George Ravenscroft, but the credit is not his alone. Ravenscroft was a specialist whose interest did not extend beyond the nature and quality of the metal, and the problems of design and craftsmanship and marketing he left to those who were expert in these different fields. His aim could not have been reached without the assistance of others, including skilled craftsmen and learned scientists; but, most of all, his success was assured by the understanding of the Glass Sellers' Company. It was the Company who supplied the funds and created the markets for his products.

The Glass Sellers' Company was directed by a group of intelligent men of affairs, who stood in the van of that modern movement which sprang from a grasp of the significance of scientific investigation and linked the discoveries of the laboratory to the work of the factory. It was these men who set a high standard of quality and were willing to spend money and time to obtain it. It was they who interpreted their customers' needs in a way never at variance with good design and good taste. And it was they whose wisdom and foresight exploited the whole situation both on the manufacturing and selling sides, thereby extending the use of glass to a new and much greater public. England owes much to such men, not only for their commercial abilities but for their artistic and moral qualities that were so much at one with the best in national character.

A few specimens of bowls, tazzas, jugs, and wineglasses stamped with the raven's head are still preserved in private collections and museums, but there is a greater number of glasses made at a later period after the seal had been withdrawn. It is impossible to say if these latter were made under Ravenscroft's management or by his successor Hawley Bishop, but, in any case, as crizzelling has become manifest in the vessels with the seal and also in some of the later specimens to a lesser extent, the glasses that come to us from the Savoy glasshouse belong to an experimental phase in the making of this particular kind of glass.

Ravenscroft's patent expired about the time of his death, and the making of flint glass thereafter extended to London manufacturers outside of the Glass Sellers' Company; and in ten years, glasshouses throughout England, and in Dublin and Scotland as well, were making flint glass, not, at first, with very happy results. Fifty years were to pass before provincial glassmakers acquired a technology equal to the high standard of London.

Before the century closed, England was exporting flint glass to the Continent, and a period of great prosperity followed in which the Government saw an opportunity to raise a little money. A tax was levied on flint glass and bottles, but the men of that generation did not accept impositions with the tameness that has become the outstanding characteristic of the citizens of our own day. There was a great to-do. Public meetings were organized, pamphlets were scattered and petitions presented. The hullabaloo was kept up for four years until the Government yielded at last and withdrew the tax. In 1746, however, taxation was again applied, this time with greater firmness, so that the industry was brought close to the brink of ruin.

THE DEVELOPMENT OF GLASSMAKING IN SCOTLAND

In Scotland the first essay in glassmaking, which was made at Wemyss in 1610 by George Hay and was continued by Sir Robert Mansell, did not survive the term of Sir Robert's life. It was not until 1698 that Lord Elcho attempted to revive the industry at Wemyss by starting a new company there. Little is known of this work or its products, however, except that it existed.

When, about 1631 or a little later, the first works at Wemyss was closed, some of the glassworkers crossed the Firth of Forth and set up in Leith and in the adjacent village of Prestonpans. In this they were actuated by an old tradition of their craft to follow the market, for Leith, the port for Edinburgh, was at that time the center of a very considerable trade in wines, and it was natural, perhaps inevitable, that glassmaking should be established there to supply the bottles necessary for the retail distribution of wine.

The industry began there before the latter half of the seventeenth century and was certainly established by 1661, for John Ray, an English naturalist who traveled through Scotland in that year, records that he saw glass being made at Prestonpans "from a mixture of kelp, salt and local sand all calcined and melted in ovens."

It is likely that this venture, too, ended in failure and that a number of foreign craftsmen were doomed to idleness. At any rate a new works was started by William Morrison about 1697. This was called *Morrison's Haven.* The name is surely significant. It might have arisen spontaneously from the thankful hearts of starving glassmakers to whom the prospect of employment must have broken through the darkness of their tribulation as the joy that "cometh in the morning." On the other hand, and equally possible, the name may have been an ironic comment made by parochial onlookers who would incline to regard foreign glassworkers, with their alien ways and strolling propensities, as little better than vagrants. If this conjecture is near the truth, then "Haven" is one of the flowers of a dry humor, typical of the Scots of that day, indicating that Morrison's neighbors thought more of his heart than his head, and that this judgment did nothing to raise him in their esteem.

By this time native workers were beginning to take an interest in the craft, although foreigners were still indispensable. Even as late as 1696 two Edinburgh men, William Montgomerie and George Linn, were given a license for "a pot-house and all conveniences for making glass and for bringing home from foreign countries men required for such work."

This suggests that native craftsmen were either not numerous or not up to the work, and that few of the sons of the original foreign glassworkers at Wemyss remained in the country. It may be, of course, that these sons and grandsons of foreigners had never been out of Scotland and so had lost the cunning of their sires by their separation from the progressive glassmaking centers in England and Europe.

But it was never difficult to induce foreign craftsmen to come to Scotland apparently, so that any businessman who had a mind to set up a glasshouse was never deterred by the want of skilled workers. He had but to advertise in the Netherlands, and the response was prompt enough. This preference on the part of foreigners always puzzled Sir Robert Mansell. As long as George Hay owned the glasshouse at Wemyss he was blamed for enticing Mansell's workmen from England, and, doubtless, the accusation was not unfounded.

Yet George Hay was not wholly to blame, for when Mansell bought the Wemyss works, he imagined this trouble to be at an end, only to find that the migration still continued. "My men are again drawn into Scotland," he writes, and although he can suggest no reason for this state of affairs, it is possible that Scots character and outlook conformed more closely to the tastes and feelings of aliens, many of whom were earnest professors of the Protestant faith and stout upholders of Calvinism.

The foreigners who made their way from England to Scotland, however, were never, at any time, the best craftsmen. George Hay's products were poor, and after Mansell took over the Wemyss works the quality did not improve. It is recorded in another of Mansell's many complaints that his Scottish workers "made such ill-conditioned glass as at one time he lossed £2,000 thereby."

It was the sons and grandsons of these men upon whom Morrison depended when he erected the glasshouse at Morrison's Haven. But to their number he added others brought from the Continent, as otherwise he could not have realized his ambition to make all kinds of glass, including mirrors and lead glass, the making of which demanded difficult techniques. For making mirrors he employed Paul le Blanc, a Frenchman who had become a naturalized subject. Le Blanc was assisted by his son and by William Scott, both able and, indeed, outstanding craftsmen.

Hitherto Scottish attempts to make mirrors consisted of fixing tin foil to a sheet of glass, but Morrison improved this method by using tin foil in conjunction with mercury, a new technique that was to remain supreme for the next hundred years. The technique was not without its drawbacks, however, for the weight of the coating often fractured the plate, and drops of mercury caused streaks in the reflecting surface. The operation, too, had bad effects on the health of the workers.

Morrison was rewarded by the success of his undertaking, and there is little doubt that the progress of the craft in Scotland owes something to him. It would be possible to overestimate his importance, however. A paragraph, for instance, in a contemporary newspaper claims that:

"Their mirrors and other pieces of work exceed any that come from abroad."

This statement leans perhaps towards national prejudice, and before accepting it wholeheartedly one would like to know from what source the writer derived his information. That it came from an interview with Morrison himself seems likely, and, if that is so, we may take it that the judgment is not impartial. Nevertheless, Morrison did succeed in giving to Scotland some good glass and mirrors of a quality superior to anything that had been produced in that country before.

By 1695 the industry had become established in Edinburgh and Leith, where a hundred and twenty blowers were engaged in addition to their numerous attendants. Within five years glassmaking was to extend to Glasgow, and before the close of the eighteenth century to Alloa, Perth, and Dundee. The industry, however, was without the discipline of a monitor such as the Glass Sellers' Company, and time was to pass before Scottish Glass approached the high standard of London. Nevertheless, at the end of the seventeenth century the glass being made in Scotland was good enough for the English market.

Chapter Seven

GERMAN GLASS

STYLES IN GERMAN GLASSMAKING

AT the time when Ravenscroft was experimenting with lead glass, experiments were also being made in Germany to find a substitute for Venetian *cristallo*. These resulted in a heavy, clear glass produced by adding carbonate of lime, in the form of chalk, to the batch. As this glass had an indirect but important influence in glassmaking throughout Europe and in England as well, the circumstances leading to its discovery should not be overlooked. An immediate consequence of this new glass was to develop the arts of engraving and glass cutting, which, in Germany, had declined and fallen away since Roman times.

It is true that engraving had been revived during the early seventeenth century in Germany, and that good work was done in the thin Venetian glass of the times, but the full development of engraving and cutting was not possible until a thicker and more substantial glass was available, so that it was not until the second half of the seventeenth century that glass engraving and cutting became fully established in Bohemia, Silesia, and Potsdam.

Later, about the middle of the nineteenth century, the best of German glass cutting and engraving again achieved new heights in a completely different mode of artistic expression which was to have widespread influence on glassmaking throughout Europe, England, and even America. For that reason a knowledge of German glassmaking is desirable if not necessary, and for that reason a very brief review of the development of the art in Germany is now made here.

In glassmaking the term "German" implies work done not in Germany alone but in the Germanic countries as well. It covers glassmaking in northern and middle Europe, in Germany itself, in Austria, and in Bohemia. As with the rest of Europe, German glass during the Dark Ages and in the Middle Ages was an art that had been given by Roman civilization and was one practiced almost exclusively by strolling bands of Syrians or Egyptians.

But these foreign craftsmen could not remain in the countries of their adoption without becoming influenced by the outlook and feelings of those among whom they lived. In Germany, perhaps more than elsewhere, one can see the effects of national influence upon these craftsmen in the change from low, Roman shapes, conceived like classical architecture in horizontal planes, to the tapering, slender designs that follow the vertical lines of the Gothic.

The metal produced in Germany during the Middle Ages was the green or yellow or brown natural forest glass, or *Waldglas*, made from an alkali derived from ferns or beechwood. Among the earliest forms of German glass is a low palm-cup. This is simply an ovoid cup without handles, having a kick-up in the base. From this low cup, designs gradually became taller, rising in height to the proportions of the cone and claw beakers which have already been discussed,[1] and branching into varieties of the slender, cylinder-shaped vessels that were to become the forerunners of the fine so-called *Spechter* glasses for which fifteenth- and sixteenth-century German glassmakers were renowned.

Among German drinking glasses of the fifteenth century are three important developments—the *Römer*, the *Krautstrunk*, and the *Spechter*. At one time the origin of the word *Römer* was believed to have come from Roman, or from the fact that glasses of this kind were used in the *Römersaal* at Frankfurt, but these views are no longer accepted. The name *Römer*, W. B. Honey tells us in *Glass*, the handbook of the Victoria and Albert Museum collection, is perhaps taken from the Lower Rhenish *roeman*, to boast. Nevertheless, just sufficient uncertainty exists to make the point an agreeable bone of contention among learned persons for a long time to come, if not, indeed, for all time.

The *Römer* did not reach full development until the seventeenth

[1] See pages 32 and 34.

century. Long after clear glass was available, glassmakers in Germany still continued to make *Römers* in an attractive green metal similar to the traditional *Waldglas*. Early specimens may be tall or short, with small blobs of glass, called prunts, applied to the surface of the lower portion. Sometimes these prunts were smooth, sometimes pointed, and in later examples were often impressed with a design so they look like raspberries. Ravenscroft, in England, made *Römers* decorated with prunts like strawberries. Specimens of these exist in the Wilfred Buckley collection. The feet of early *Römers* were formed by coiling a trail of hot glass into a conical shape. Later a hollow blown foot appeared on some examples, and in the eighteenth and nineteenth centuries a trail of glass was wound around the hollow blown foot to make it appear like a coiled, trailed foot. In recent years, this effect has been accomplished on the feet of *Römers*, a form which is still being made, by the use of a mold.

The *Krautstrunk*—that is to say, a cabbage runt—or as it is also called, a *Warzenbecher* or *Nuppenbecher*, is nothing more than a small, barrel-shaped beaker decorated with applied thorn-like prunts and supported on a crimped foot. From the number of surviving examples it was apparently a popular drinking vessel. The deep green of the unrefined metal combined with this simple form and decoration result in a form highly pleasing to the eye as well as practical in a day when forks for dining were unknown.

The type often called *Spechter* is a glass of a different form, being cylindrical with tapered sides with overall applied and molded decoration in the form of a series of raised squares spiraling upwards from base to rim. This decoration seems to have been done by applying a broad spiral trail of glass onto the surface of the partly blown vessel, then inserting it into a mold with vertical ribs and expanding the gather, thus forming an overall pattern of squares. These *Spechters*, often made of blue as well as light green glass, were usually further decorated by a series of simple colored enamel dots and gilding between the raised squares.

Through the *Römer*, the *Krautstrunk* and the *Spechter*, Germany has given to the art work that has a satisfying nobility of proportions and is something which she alone could give. While the claw beaker arose from Syrian genius giving expression to feelings that were Teutonic, the *Römer* and its fellows are the outcome of German genius speaking for itself.

Other styles that developed along with the *Römer* and that were no less German in inspiration include the *Kuttrolf* or *Angster*, the *Stangenglas*, the *Igel*, the *Passglas*, the *Willkomm* and the *Humpen*. In addition, a somewhat crude taste was exuberantly expressed through a perplexing variety of puzzle glasses and glasses in the shape of women, bears, pigs, boots, hats and other forms with a strong appeal to a hearty, bucolic sense of fun.

Kuttrolf or *Angster* vessels were descendants of the slow-pouring Roman *Gutturnium*, used for pouring costly oils and perfumes (*Plate 26*). In the seventeenth century this type of vessel was very popular for serving the more expensive kind of drinks. They had necks composed of several tubes twisted about each other. The name *Kuttrolf* is echoic and is said to imitate the gurgling sound made when these vessels were being poured, but it is possible that the name could be derived from the Roman word *Gutturnium*.

Stange is the German word for a pole or rod, and *Stangengläser* were so named because of their tall, cylindrical shape. As a rule the earliest glasses of this kind have drops applied to the outer surface and they are of medieval origin. Later ones are usually plain, or enameled. The *Igel* is a rather similar glass, but has the knops drawn to a point so that, as the name implies, the glass resembles a hedgehog. In the *Passglas* is a reminder of an old drinking custom. This tall cylindrical beaker is divided into equal portions by applied or enameled rings. When one had imbibed the contents down to the first ring the glass was passed to the crony with whom one shared the loving pot. He then drank down to the next ring, passed the glass back and so on down to the lees. How useful such a glass might have been to those two Dickensian topers, Sarah Gamp and Betsy Prig! And how it would have saved Sarah the trouble of continually issuing the inhibitory warning:

"Drink fair, Betsy, drink fair!"

A variation of the *Passglas* is the *Bandwurmglas* (*Plate 27*), which has a notched trail applied in a spiral to its surface. *Willkomm*, the cup of welcome or greeting glass, is a variant of the *Stangenglas* and from it was derived the capacious *Humpen* so popular in Germanic countries from the sixteenth and seventeenth centuries and continuing in use through the nineteenth century.

Plate 26 GERMAN SEVENTEENTH CENTURY GLASS
Kuttrolf or *Angster*. The body with applied trails pinched into diamond patterns, the neck composed of three intertwined tubes which open to form a trefoil mouth. A white enamel twist is enclosed in the rim.
[*The Royal Scottish Museum, Edinburgh*]

Plate 27 GERMAN GLASS
This Rhenish *Bandwurmglas* of the sixteenth century is a reminder of an ancient social custom when two people shared the same glass.
[*Victoria and Albert Museum photograph. Crown Copyright*]

ENAMELED GLASS

The application of enamel colors to glass, derived from the Venetians but of a completely different character, was practiced by the Germans with great vigor. In the late sixteenth and early seventeenth centuries this craft was centered in Bohemia whence it spread to Hesse and Brandenburg. At that time it was in essence a peasant art, interesting rather than beautiful, whose main attraction rested in a strong, vital quality. The colors used were opaque and not always particularly suited in conjunction with clear glass. The subjects included landscapes, armorials, especially of the Holy Roman Empire, biblical subjects, scenes of craftsmen at work, and satirical pieces whose treatment often revealed a robust but coarse sense of humor (*Plate 28*).

Towards the end of the sixteenth century enamels were applied to a blue glass in Bohemia. A good representative collection of these is to be seen in the Victoria and Albert Museum, and at least one specimen of *Fichtelgebirge* enameled glass is held in the British Museum. Thuringian enameling was done near Coburg, and the style of painting an outline on the outside of the glass and filling it with washes applied to the inside of the glass began there. Hessian enameled glass may sometimes be distinguished by the green or yellowish-green glass upon which the colors were applied.

The enameled glass of Saxony is perhaps on a higher level. Much of the work there was concerned with armorial glasses of which the metal was clear and of good quality, the enamel colors very lively. Among the most outstanding glasses from Saxony are the *Hallorengläser*, which were made for the guild of salt workers of Halle-an-der-Saale.

This peasant art does not represent a very important development in glass. The good thing about it was that it was hearty and robust, but it did not lead to any very distinguished artistic expression or reveal much sensitive feeling on the part of those concerned. The drawing is often commonplace, the coloring crude, and the choice of subject frequently betrays a lack of refinement. A man standing on a ladder to enable him to embrace a very tall woman, for instance, is a topic more likely to give scope for Rabelaisian wit than to engender elegant feeling. Not that there is anything wrong with Rabelaisian wit in its right place; and if a drinking party is its right place, then glasses decorated in this way were not, after all, altogether inapposite.

About the middle period of the seventeenth century a Nuremberg stained-glass artist, Johann Schaper, discovered a new style of decorating glass with enamel called *Schwarzlot*. *Schwarzlot* was done mostly in black with points of red and gold, and it became a popular treatment for house windows as well as for vessels. Schaper was a freelance who painted pottery as well as glass and he has left a considerable number of signed pieces. By the early eighteenth century the fashion was taken up in Bohemia and Silesia, and was practiced there both by established glasshouses and independent artists.

An important development that took place in the eighteenth century was that of *Zwischengoldgläser* (*Plate 29*), a revival, but a variation, of the Roman technique of laminating a layer of gold leaf with a design scratched in it between two layers of glass. In the Roman period the two layers of glass were fused together with heat, while at this time the outer and inner walls of the vessel were closely fitted together and, after the design had been made in the gold, were cemented together. Usually the top quarter-inch or so of the inner section was left the same thickness as the thickness of the combined walls of the two sections, so that it projected and came in line with the outer section when it was slipped over the inner wall, thus forming a solid rim for the vessel. This technique demanded great care and patience, and that painstaking thoroughness which is one of the outstanding virtues of German character. The subject matter of these *Zwischengoldgläser* was often hunt scenes, but religious portrayals, portraits, and monograms were also popular. At their best, examples of this type of work represent a delicate art executed with fine spirit and superb skill.

ENGRAVED GLASS

As in England during the seventeenth century, Venetian clear glass and Venetian designs and treatment held supremacy in Germany and, like the English, Germans were longing for a similar glass of their own that could be made from the materials to be found within their own frontiers. This wish resulted in a number of experiments that led to the discovery of a new type of

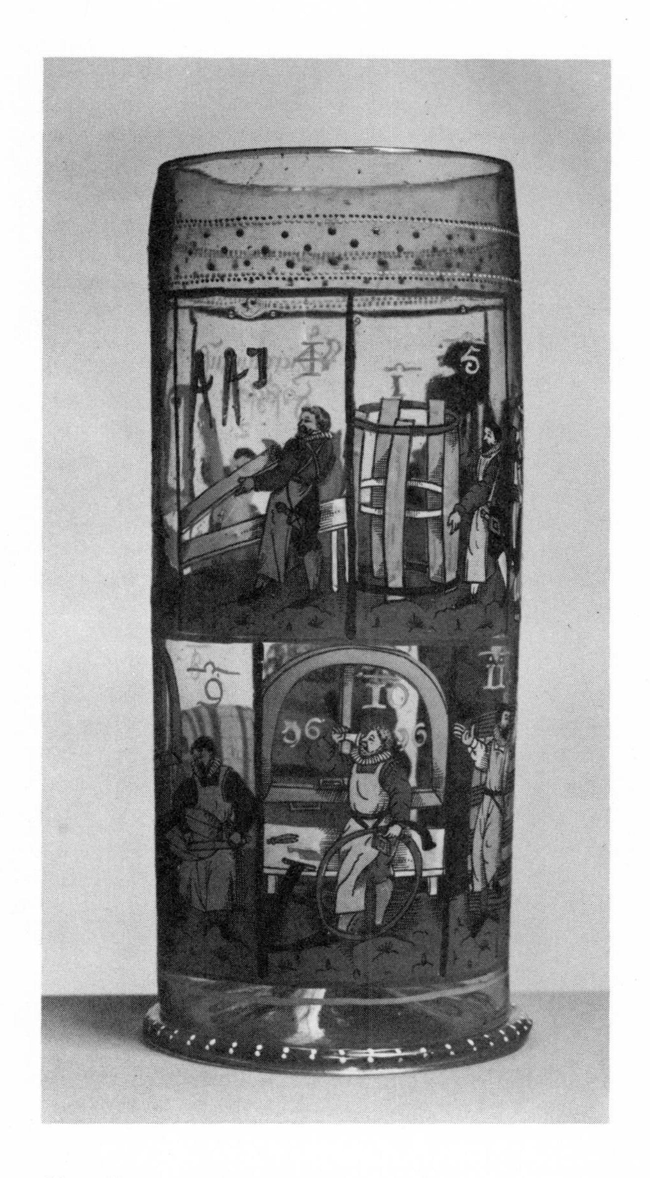

Plate 28 GERMAN GLASS
This glass, painted in enamel colors, illustrates the vigor and humor of a peasant art. This specimen is dated 1616.
[*Victoria and Albert Museum photograph. Crown Copyright*]

Plate 29 ZWISCHENGOLDGLAS BEAKER
Probably made in Bohemia about 1730. [*The Corning Museum of Glass*]

glass, and it happened that the quest was being made at the time Ravenscroft was making his experiments in England. Like him, German glassmakers had set out deliberately to discover a new formula that would produce a glass equal if not superior to Venetian *cristallo*.

It was in Bohemia, about 1680, the year before Ravenscroft died, that the new glass became possible. The composition of this new glass included a large proportion of chalk, and the use of potash replaced soda. A very good, clear glass was obtained that had a hard brilliance when cut, although it fell short of the high standard attained in English lead glass and was without the same elusive beauty and inner fire. Apparently the new formula was not kept secret, for the fashion spread quickly and soon reached every glasshouse throughout the country.

The development of the new glass followed a course rather similar to that taken by lead glass in England. It was met by corresponding obstacles and subject to the same defects. At first the glass was used in the Venetian manner, which depended for its decorative treatment on the application of trails, on the use of pincer work, and on the free manipulation of the vessel in its plastic state. The glass, however, could be blown much thicker than Venetian *cristallo* and it was not long before its possibilities for a glyptic treatment were realized.

As it turned out, the glass was particularly suited for deep facet cutting and wheel engraving. As the cutting of gems and semi-precious stones was an art very popular in Germany at that time, it is little wonder that skilled lapidarists should turn their attention to this new medium that offered scope for their talents.

The art of glass cutting and engraving flourished with great vigor henceforth and continued until the closing years of the eighteenth century, being practiced by numerous artists whose names are long since forgotten. But perhaps the period owes more to several eminent glass engravers of whom were numbered Friedrich Winter, who worked at Petersdorf in the Hirschberg Tal, his brother Martin, and Gottfried Spiller and Heinrich Jäger, all of Berlin, and Franz Gundelach.

Each of these artists was expert in *Hochschnitt* or cameo-relief and *Tiefschnitt* or intaglio work, and each brought to the advancement of the art something of his own. Certainly it is due to them that the baroque style through which they expressed themselves was brought to a level not much short of perfection. Specimens of Spiller's work, and work done in the Gundelach manner, are included in the collection of the Victoria and Albert Museum.

For a time German engraved glass was pre-eminent, and of all the engraving centers those of Bohemia and Silesia were predominant. Silesian work became outstanding for vessels made in flower-petal forms, shell patterns, scrolls, and palmette foliage in the rococo style, most of which was executed by artists whose names are now forgotten. Among the engravers working in Nuremberg was Anton Wilhelm Mäuerl, who visited England for a short time where he practiced his art.

In Berlin, Gundelach and Spiller were followed by a number of artists including Halter, Rosbach, and Bode, whose work appealed to the Prussian taste for military subjects done in bold outlines and massive forms. But in less gifted artists (and they were many) this predilection for heaviness often resulted in an aggressive masculinity and a depressing absence of grace.

In the eighteenth century an opaque-white glass gained great popularity in Germany. This lent itself to a painted decoration in the manner of porcelain. A similar glass was produced in Venice,[1] but the Germans extended the use of this for making cups and saucers decorated with colored designs. Large quantities of this ware were exported.

Towards the close of the eighteenth century the influence of English glass exerted itself in Germany. English lead glass was particularly suited for facet cutting, for the prismatic surfaces of this style revealed to the best advantage that attractive quality, at once soft and brilliant, that is the outstanding characteristic of this glass. Inspired by English example, the Germans took to facet cutting, and their taste for the airy styles of the rococo gave place to simpler forms better suited to this form of decoration.

The change was in keeping with the times, however, just as Fragonard and Watteau were followed by David and the Neo-Classic school of the Empire period. The Empire period was but a step, perhaps an inevitable one, to the Gothic Revival with its sentimental warmth and misdirected enthusiasm. Glassmaking did not escape the craze for imitating medieval models, and in Germany this romantic indulgence culminated in the appalling

[1] See page 40.

ineptitude achieved by the Munich school of stained-glass artists, whose too enduring work and influence now disfigure so much church architecture not only in Germany but in England as well.

In the period that followed the Napoleonic wars commercial prosperity brought wealth, power, and increase to the middle class, whose standard of taste at that time was not restrained by innate refinement or formed by education. Nevertheless, this rising class of manufacturers and shopkeepers, entering into unaccustomed luxury, hankered after the symbols of a cultured way of life. They had the money to indulge their fancy and were the kind of men who knew what they liked and were willing to pay for it. Glassmakers, along with other caterers of elegant living, responded to the call to give the customer what he wanted.

Giving the customer what he wants, however, is a policy fraught with danger for the artist. Too often it results in debased forms of art which, in turn, produces a spiritual deterioration in the artists themselves, so that they become, at last, stale and incapable of vital expression.

This period in Germany was known as the *Biedermeierzeit*, a term that might be rendered as the Era of the Would-be Gentleman. One of its effects on glass was to cut short the fashion of cut crystal and to replace that fashion with one of colored glass usually made in massive forms of bad proportions. This was accompanied by a revival of the craze that had been the besetting sin of glassmakers in the Middle Ages, of making glass to imitate semi-precious stones, and the bad habit, not so long outgrown, threatened to creep back like a maggot into the glassmaker's brain. Of this type of glass an opaque black glass called "Hyalith" and an opaque glass of streaked colors called "Lithalin" were the most famous.

A popular type of cutting was done on colored glass cased either with white or a contrasting color. The surface casing was cut away with a wheel in designs of conventional patterns, and thus the different colors of the glass beneath the top layer were revealed, somewhat in the manner of the Roman *diatretarii* which we have already noted.

This technique was used by a number of engravers for pictorial subjects. A beaker or other vessel, for example, might be decorated in this way with some romantic scene of the locality, and as such was prized as a memento by a foreign visitor who, in nine cases out of ten, would be English. For that reason German glass of this period is to be picked up now and again throughout Europe and England. The most outstanding engraver of this period was Dominik Biemann (*Plate 31*) whose work is rare and highly prized.

Now it is all very well for a better instructed generation to look down its nose at the *Biedermeierzeit*, or sniff at Victorianism, but the time was not without some good. For one thing it was vigorous, if more than a little vulgar. Also, it encouraged the technology of colored glass; and if the cheaper products were clumsy and crude, the more costly things were fashioned with exquisite skill and, even if we now think that skill might have been applied with more restraint and better taste, it was still skill of a high order.

Thus German glass in the artistic field presents a perplexing variety of styles and great profusion of production. It ranges from ludicrous extravagance to dignified simplicity, from utter bathos to excellence achieved by superb skill. If there is one fault that is general throughout the many different styles of expression it is in a too conscious striving after originality and an overweening desire to impress.

But however German glass may vary on the artistic side, the quality of the metal is usually very high, a satisfactory result achieved by the skill of German technologists among whom should be mentioned the pioneer chemist Johann Kunckel. Kunckel worked at Potsdam. Like Ravenscroft in England, he succeeded in producing a clear glass of exceptional quality which later developed crizzelling due to excess of alkali. He produced, too, many colored glasses of fine quality, including a fine ruby-colored glass, frequently engraved and fitted with gilt mountings.

His life was not without trials nor he without enemies. When his patron, the Elector Friedrich Wilhelm, died, his foes conspired against him, burnt his glasshouse to the ground, and forced him to give up his connection with the industry in Potsdam. After that incident he visited Sweden, but ten years before his death his services were recognized and he was ennobled and became Kunckel von Löwenstern. The world owes much to those German chemists who turned their attention to glass and not least to that able pioneer, Johann Kunckel.

Plate 30
A Bohemian glass jug about the middle of the nineteenth century.
[*Victoria and Albert Museum photograph. Crown Copyright*]

Plate 31 DOMINIK BIEMANN MEDALLION
Portrait of an unidentified man engraved by Dominik Biemann and dated 1834.
[*The Corning Museum of Glass*]

Chapter Eight

EIGHTEENTH-CENTURY GLASS IN ENGLAND

NEW STANDARDS IN ENGLISH TASTE

IN England at the opening of the eighteenth century there was a reaction against gaudiness and excessive ornamental adornment. In architecture the followers of Inigo Jones in the Palladian style, influenced by Lord Shaftesbury, set a fashion for plainness expressed in the pleasing proportions of classical lines. The taste of the times, which we associate with the reign of Queen Anne, influenced design in many arts, including furniture, silver, and glass.

It happened that the heaviness of lead glass, then coming into use, was admirably suited to the classical style. The glass had great brilliance and richness, and these qualities were seen to the best advantage when they were allowed to speak for themselves and were not hidden by the intricate flourishes of a baroque treatment which, in fact, was more suited to a thinly blown glass like *cristallo*.

In any case it was time for the pendulum to swing. The baroque style had held the field for long enough, and fashion was thirsting for a change. It was perhaps not unnatural that this change should begin in England, for while the baroque style had always had a wholehearted acceptance in Italy, this was not so in England where national character was more properly expressed in a kind of solid stateliness that was at once unpretentious and graceful. Indeed, this genuine quality persisted and made itself felt even when the baroque style was in the zenith of its popularity.

The greater number of middle-class people in England may have accounted for this state of affairs. Baroque designs were best expressed in a fluid glass, like *cristallo*, that could be blown very thin. It was not glass that endured, however, nor was it meant to. It was the kind of glass that was made for some special occasion, and most of it was smashed during the course of the entertainment for which it had been expressly designed. Baroque, therefore, was made for the rich and influential, who could order new glasses in more fantastic shapes when the next occasion came round. Extravagance of this kind was beyond the reach of the middle class, and, indeed, was repugnant to them, so that, even had they been able to indulge themselves in this way, their instincts of frugality would have inhibited the desire before it had become conscious thought. The middle-class man and his wife were not the people to buy a new set of glasses every time they threw a party, and they would have been scandalized at the suggestion. The glass they wanted was something expected to last at least for the lifetime of the purchaser, if not to be handed on to succeeding generations.

In the seventeenth century, when baroque was the thing, the middle class was sufficiently numerous to create a considerable market. It was to cater for this market that Greene devoted much of his talent. Possibly, when he created simple shapes, he did so at first to produce inexpensive glasses having the merit of a good design likely to appeal to a discriminating taste that would be, at the same time, within the reach of middle-class buyers; but, in doing so, he was expressing something that belonged to English feeling and character. Glass, however, that depends on shape alone for its aesthetic appeal must have a certain amount of weight. It must have a substantial quality, and this was not inherent in *cristallo*. One of Greene's chief reasons for his dissatisfaction with Venetian glass was that the glassmakers in Murano would not blow vessels thickly enough. In spite of repeated complaints, the glasses made in Italy to Greene's order were always too thin, and it was not until English lead glass was discovered that the right medium was available through which English taste could be aptly expressed.

And in giving this expression, English glassmakers were guided by a sure instinct through which they reached their highest achievement. In this period of artistic awakening and heartening vitality eighteenth-century glass has a beauty and genuine quality that has never been surpassed; and after centuries of tutelage to foreign methods and ideas, the craft in England at last came into its own and was able to give something to the world which it alone could give. How much of this triumph is directly attributable to John Greene and how much to the influence of the good design ruling during the reign of Queen Anne it would be difficult to say, but certainly without Greene's preparatory work design must have taken longer to evolve along the particular line it was destined to take; and without Greene's touch of genius it is doubtful if it could have arisen so aptly and spontaneously to the occasion.

Greene, as we have seen, was a London importer of Venetian glass who, dissatisfied with Italian designs, started to draw designs for himself that were more in keeping with English feeling; but the Italian workmen in Murano were unable, perhaps incapable, of producing these designs in glass in a way to satisfy his exacting standards.[1] Although experience pointedly and persistently suggested otherwise, he seemed to believe that these standards were attainable, as, indeed, they were when carried out in the heavier medium of lead glass and fashioned by English workmen, so that his faith was justified in the end.

The period that followed in the late seventeenth century and the first half of the eighteenth was one of great expansion and activity in which Greene's ideas were to take effect in a great variety of detail, the most perplexing of which, from the collector's point of view, is to be found in the stems of wineglasses. It is with this period that most private collections begin, but it is in this period that the classification of stems becomes more than difficult. Many learned men have drawn up categories to enable collectors to build up a collection in series, but none has wholly succeeded. Today the classification given by W. A. Thorpe in his *A History of English and Irish Glass* is generally accepted as the most reliable guide. In *English Table Glass*, E. M. Elville gives the more usual forms from this classification in the following sequence, although he points out that the dates are not necessarily those given by Thorpe.

Baluster Stems	
Inverted Baluster	1682–1710
Drop Knop	1690–1710

[1] See pages 62–64.

Angular Knop	1695–1715
Ball Knop	1695–1715
Annulated or Triple Ring Knop	1700–1725
Multiple Knops	1700–1720
True Baluster	1710–1730
Acorn Knop	1710–1715
Mushroom Knop	1710–1715

In Greene's drawings the bowls of wineglasses are capacious and the stems short, these being, in fact, a single knop usually hollow, called by Greene a "wrought button," which might be ribbed or plain. The foot curves upward with an inward sweep to meet the button, and the whole glass is unadorned but beautiful in its fine proportions. This single button stem was the beginning of the baluster, and, as time goes on, we find stems becoming longer, bowls less capacious, and a more sophisticated style developing.

At first the button was elongated so that it lost its spherical shape. Then it was tapered upward to form an inverted baluster and, lastly, tapered downward to form a true baluster. In the rudimentary stage the baluster is squat (*Plate 32*), then it becomes longer and is attached to a rather smaller bowl. Inverted balusters were much more popular than real balusters until waisted bowls became fashionable about 1710. Then the real baluster came into its own, for it is admirably adapted to this particular combination. And so, through many gradations and endless formations, Greene's low shapes and heavy glass evolve into a tall, vertical, and lighter style.

In the earlier evolutionary stages of the baluster stem are glasses with hollow knop stems in which is enclosed a coin. From the dates of these coins it is clear that such glasses were made as late as 1776 although the fashion came in about 1690. The Victoria and Albert Museum includes in its collection some admirable examples of these.

After the Treaty of Utrecht in 1713 and following the accession to the Throne of George I in 1714, German craftsmen came to settle in England, bringing with them fresh ideas that were not without effect on English design. Among these was the Silesian stem (*Plate 32*), which, we are told, is misnamed, for the style originated in Hesse or, at any rate, in western Germany. Yet, in spite of protests from the learned, the name has persisted, but if

a, b, c

d, e, f

Plate 32 ENGLISH EXAMPLES OF SILESIAN AND BALUSTER STEMS

a Taper-stick or tea-candlestick with spirally molded Silesian stem. 1740–50.

b Wineglass with molded Silesian stem and folded foot; straight-sided bowl with solid base and cup-shaped knop. *Circa* 1720. Height $8\frac{3}{4}$ inches.

c Sweetmeat glass with molded Silesian stem. *Circa* 1730–35.

d Wineglass with waisted bell-shaped bowl, baluster stem and foot with folded rim. *Circa* 1720. Height $6\frac{1}{4}$ inches.

e Wineglass with "thistle" bowl, baluster stem with mushroom knop and folded foot. *Circa* 1710.

f Wineglass with baluster stem containing "tear." Bell-shaped bowl, folded foot. *Circa* 1720. [*The Royal Scottish Museum, Edinburgh*]

you happen to be a purist in these matters and nice in your choice of words, you may call the Silesian a molded or pedestal or shouldered stem and still be understood.

Earlier Silesian stems had four sides, being square in section. This gave place to an octagonal section and finally to a round which was ribbed vertically. The fashion as applied to wineglasses did not survive beyond the middle of the eighteenth century, although its use was continued in sweet and other dishes. Today the vertically ribbed column is often used to good effect on candlesticks.

THE GLASS EXCISE ACTS

Perhaps the most important influence, or, at any rate, the most far-reaching, was that exerted by the Glass Excise Acts of 1745, 1777, and 1787. The tax so imposed continued for nearly a hundred years and was only repealed when the industry throughout the country had been reduced to a state little short of ruin. The restriction was made at a time when the craft was showing great vigor and enterprise, and the tax proved to be a piece of legislative folly that did considerable harm to the economy of the nation. There is every reason to suppose that glassmakers were then entering a phase of what might have been unprecedented prosperity had they been allowed freedom. In the hundred years following 1745 many towns, particularly in England, increased to more than double their former size. The production of bricks in this period of expansion increased by ninety per cent, whereas the increase in glass production in the same period did not reach two per cent.

Flint glass was taxed by weight, at a penny for every pound, and the duty was applied when the metal was in the pot or, as the Act says, "at the furnace mouth." As no allowance was made for breakage during the later stages of manufacture or during transport from works to warehouse, the tax was an even greater imposition than it seemed at first sight.

The duty, too, was most rigorously applied. An excise officer was constantly in attendance in each works, the pots for melting the glass had now to be of a specified size and shape, and these were registered after their capacity had been calculated. During working hours the exciseman was always to be found hanging about the glasshouse, gauging the contents of the pots from time to time with an iron rod, and a fine of £200 was the penalty for changing any marks made by him. It was all done with great thoroughness.

The lehr, too, was under his vigilant eye. This had also to conform to a specified rectangular design, having only one entrance and one exit, and each of these had to have doors furnished with locks. In this way evasion of the tax was impossible for any glassmaker with law-abiding principles and a sense of citizenship, but to the less conscientious, the regulations encouraged abuse. Arnold Fleming, in *Scottish and Jacobite Glass*, tells us that a black market in glass began to be organized, and in Scotland this was of no mean scope.

The back courts of Edinburgh provided an admirable cover for small, illicit glasshouses, where cullet, or broken and scrap glass, formed a raw material to be melted and fashioned into a variety of utensils. Quite a lively business was done in this way very difficult for the authorities to detect, for retail distribution was effected not through shops and warehouses but by hawkers who roamed the countryside on foot carrying bundles on their backs. In eighteenth-century Scotland these hawkers were a numerous band, an accepted part of the social order, on whose individual excursions it would have been impossible to keep any check.

The duties on glass were collected by the department of the excise that looked after wines and spirits, a circumstance that accounts for the conjunction of the words "Glaziers and Vintners," often to be met with in old documents. Like Gilbert's policeman, the excise officer's lot was not a happy one. His presence in the glasshouse was resented by masters and workmen alike, and things were made hot for him in a very literal sense.

Nothing was easier than the arrangement for little accidents which his hovering presence at the furnace mouth made a positive temptation. Holes were burned in his clothes by falling particles of hot glass, he was ostracized, became the victim of practical jokes and was the butt of every larking apprentice, to the extent that few men would apply for such an unenviable post and the authorities had difficulty in recruiting officers in sufficient numbers. Poor fellow! He was known as the "Watch Dog," and the little sentry box into which he retired when his interfering labors permitted was called the "Dog-Hole." The misery of his existence was brought to an end in 1845, when the Act was repealed by force of public opinion.

One of the effects of this legislation was to bring in a much lighter type of glass, or rather a glass more thinly blown, and consequently to bring about changes in design. Since the tax was calculated on the weight of the metal, glassmakers were forced to use less glass in order to produce articles at prices that would not entirely prohibit sales. That meant thinner blowing and dispensing with the decorative features applied by the glassmaker during the plastic, formative stages of manufacture; but, to balance this poverty of enrichment, the better-class work came to be cut or engraved, and it was at this time that these arts became firmly established not only in London but throughout the provinces. Some enameling was also attempted, the most notable examples being provided by the Beilby family of Newcastle; but this art had really little appeal to English taste and, as it lacked the popularity of cut or engraved glass, it did not survive.

So far as the glassmaker was concerned, the period was one of continual changes forced on him by the desire to produce something of artistic merit that would yet be low enough in price to sell in the market, and in the attempt many different styles were devised only to be thrown aside for something less costly to produce.

Classification in this period, therefore, is most difficult. In wineglass stems the tendency was to make lighter balusters, and these in turn gave place to stems composed of a number of knops or buttons, placed one upon the other, and arranged in a great variety of ways. This tendency was manifest before the tax came into force, however, and was a development of the rococo style that came from France, so that lighter glass was inevitable in any case. It is not always easy to differentiate between these lighter knopped stems and the light balusters that were a feature of Newcastle glass. W. A. Thorpe, however, has given the name *balustroids* to stems of the knopped style to distinguish them from light balusters, and the definition will be found a very helpful one.

Since Mansell's time Newcastle had been a center of glassmaking, but it was in the eighteenth century that the glassmakers there attained to their greatest mastery. John Williams of Stourbridge took over the works at Closegate, and it is to him that the credit of originating the light baluster style is given. Indeed, the industry at Newcastle enjoyed a lively prosperity at that time and was able to command a fair export trade.

Newcastle glass was popular in Holland, where Dutch engravers found the soft but brilliant metal an admirable medium for their skill. A Dutch engraver, called Greenwood, was stippling Newcastle glass with a diamond point as early as 1728, and at the close of the century another engraver, Wolff, was using glass from the same source and using the same technique. Greenwood's work has the attractiveness of great delicacy. His stippling is as elusive as a passing breath and is something that attains the highest expression of this particular technique.

English glass during the first half of the eighteenth century is remarkable for its simplicity and a cool, dignified beauty that depends little, if at all, on applied decoration. The quality of the glass then was good. It contained great quantities of lead and was a heavy metal used in a substantial way. The feet of wineglasses, for instance, were folded over the edge to give durability, the bases of the bowls were solid, and the general effect was one of strength, but of strength tempered with kindliness. At no period has English character been more aptly expressed in glass, and the distinguished and restful pieces of this period are surely an outstanding contribution to the art which only the English could give.

But changes were to take place, for no art can remain always in the same place and expect to live. In this case the change was brought about by the imposition of a tax, or at any rate the change was hastened by that imposition, for there can be little doubt that the influence of the rococo style must have had its effects in any case. The tax merely brought things to a head; it did not condition the nature of the change except by creating certain limits and, as it happened, rococo was adapted to these limits. But had these limits never existed, rococo would still have held the field.

The effect of the tax, which was calculated on weight, was to encourage the production of a lighter, more "watery" glass with less lead in its composition. Less glass, too, was used in the making of a vessel, so that, in better work, the value of a glass tended more and more to be in the decoration added after the vessel had been made rather than in the glass itself; and from 1745 a new style was becoming apparent which was soon to become a popular fashion.

PLAIN-STEMMED GLASSES

To the man who has a number of baluster stems in his collection, glasses with plain stems do not hold much interest, but the plain-stemmed glasses, which were made for common use, are not to be despised. They should be valued for their own sake, for, indeed, they have comeliness and a very attractive genuine quality.

These glasses, designed for use in taverns and other places of public entertainment, were made in a substantial style to stand rough usage. They were made, too, in patterns that were easily and quickly repeated so that they were inexpensive. For speed in the manufacturing operations they were of two pieces only, the bowl and stem being one piece and the foot the other. At first sight it might seem that a restricted operation of this kind must limit variety, but this was not so. The variety of these glasses, in fact, is very wide.

Plain-stemmed wineglasses became popular about the mid-eighteenth century, and are of the type called "drawn stem," in which the stem is formed by being drawn out of the same gather of glass as the bowl. Usually the bowl of such glasses is trumpet-shaped, or waisted, and frequently contains a tear drop, or air bubble. This seems to have led quickly to the development of the air twist stem, but the former was not displaced by it. The feet on the majority of both these types of wineglasses are usually plain, and slightly sloping. Altogether these glasses have a massive and rather stately appearance.

Varieties in bowl forms such as the bucket, the ogee, and the round funnel came a little later and probably coincided with the imposition of the tax in 1745. At any rate bowls became less capacious although the length of the stem was not reduced. It was at this time that the air twist stem first appeared, but before discussing this feature let us see how this *tour de force* of the English glassmaker was brought about.

To do so it is necessary to return to Greene. It will be remembered that Greene's chief complaint about Venetian glass was that it was too thin; but when Ravenscroft produced lead glass this fault was removed by the English glassmakers. The first essays in lead glass, however, were not entirely satisfactory as the desired thickness was still not attained. It was not until the glassmaker took a second gathering of glass that the real remedy was found for this fault of lightness. In old records there are references to "single flint" and "double flint," and one supposes this means glasses made with a single gathering and those to which a second gathering had been applied.

When lead glass first came into use both single and double flint glasses were being made and both apparently were equally popular. Today, however, specimens of single flint glass are very rare. As time went on, double flint glasses gained in popularity to the extent that the making of single flint glass was discontinued. Double flint glasses were more expensive, of course, but in spite of their higher cost, they sold better because they were considered by users as the better value. They were stronger, more durable, and less likely to succumb to accidents. And apart from these practical advantages, the thicker glass was artistically right, for it fitted so well the sober modeling which was in accord with the taste of the times.

The tear enclosed in the stem of these wineglasses was a feature made possible by the double flint technique. Who discovered this attractive form of decoration is unknown, but the operation is a comparatively simple one. The glassmaker had only to make a little hollow in the soft glass of the first layer by pressing into it an iron pin. When the second layer was applied, air was trapped in the hollow and this quickly expanded with the heat to form a bubble. If the stem was then drawn out, the bubble lengthened with it and became pear-shaped.

It is easy to see how this simple idea was elaborated, first by having a number of tears instead of one, and then, later, to twist the stem to produce the spiral known as "air twist." As we have seen, almost every technique in glassmaking was known to some extent in the Roman periods, although some, but by no means all, were in rudimentary stages that were to be improved and elaborated in later ages. The air twist, however, appears as something hitherto unknown. Moreover, its development was something belonging to English character. It was a decoration springing from English skill and genius that belonged to the art of glass and was not an imitation or adaptation of some design already expressed in silver or some other medium.

Opaque twist stems (*Plate 33*) were a development that came a little later, beginning about 1745 and continuing in fashion for

Plate 33 ENGLISH OPAQUE TWIST STEM
Goblet engraved with vine spray and bird. Opaque spiral stem. *Circa* 1765.
Height 7½ inches. [*The Royal Scottish Museum, Edinburgh*]

Plate 34

Sweetmeat glass. Double ogee bowl engraved with coronets and floral festoons; domed foot with folded rim. Height $3\frac{7}{8}$ inches.

[*The Royal Scottish Museum, Edinburgh*]

Tumbler engraved with initia
P. B. in monogram, two bir
in basket. Lower portion flute
English. Early nineteenth cen
tury. The Excise Acts brough
with them a lighter glass an
encouraged the art of en
graving.

[*The Royal Scottish Museum*
Edinburgh

the next thirty-five years. As we have seen, opaque-white thread decoration was practiced in the Roman period, and during the Renaissance the technique today called *latticinio* was developed and perfected in Venice.[1] This technique, applied to wineglass stems, accorded well with English design at that time, and the results are most attractive. So attractive, indeed, that opaque twist stems have been the subject of many modern reproductions. The beginner, therefore, is advised to be on his guard where these are concerned, and to enlist the help of a reliable adviser if he intends to buy.

It is said that over a hundred varieties of single and double opaque twist stems are known, but in addition there are stems in which white canes have been combined with an air twist. The use of colored canes, which date from 1760, is much rarer. These are sometimes done in translucent colors and sometimes in opaque, the latter being considered more valuable, but whether the one or the other, all are given a high place in collections.

Indeed, the eighteenth century offers tremendous scope in the variety of vessels made in glass. There are wineglasses, ales, sweetmeats, cruets, sillabubs, mustard pots, salvers, decanters, smelling bottles and many others, but amid this plethora the opaque-white glass of Bristol and Staffordshire should not be overlooked. A similar development took place in Italy and Germany during the eighteenth century, and, as on the Continent, Bristol and opaque-white glass made elsewhere in Britain was fashioned and decorated in the manner of porcelain (*Plate 35*).

For many years collectors and authors attributed most, if not all, of this opaque-white decorated glass to Bristol, or at most conceded that only poorer, less dense white pieces were made outside of Bristol. Such a generalized distinction is not, unfortunately, a means of distinguishing the wares of this type from one area from those of another. Most are enameled with flowers or *Chinoiserie* in imitation of china painting.

Another important development took place at Nailsea, a town not far from Bristol. There jugs and bottles were made in a black glass speckled with opaque white (*Plate 36*). Other colors such as green and blue were used in place of black, and this was treated with a *latticinio* technique or mottled. Nailsea glass was made for

[1] See pages 18 and 41–42.

use in humble surroundings, but artistically it reaches a high level. Its simple shapes and the honest craftsmanship apparent in its execution give the glass a charm distinctly its own.

GLASS CUTTING

The need to cut down the quantity of glass used in making a vessel, which was brought about by taxation, encouraged the arts which apply enrichment to the glyptic article after it has left the hands of the glassmaker, and this tendency gave glass cutting its first real opportunity in England. Since 1745, when the tax was first imposed, the art of glass cutting has made great progress and has become an important branch of glassmaking today. Glass cutting in the mid-eighteenth century, however, was not the thing it is today. The glass had to be made lighter then and this meant blowing thinner, so that deep cutting, such as is common today, was not practical, and the art was limited to the shallow style known as "flat cutting."

Artistically this limitation had its advantages. It insisted on simplicity and kept cutters from the exuberance of the overdone elaborations so much admired a century later. The shallow facet cut with a round-edge wheel, the diamond and hexagon, and plain simple grooving give to the glass of this period an attractiveness not diminished by being restrained.

GLASSMAKING IN IRELAND

Another important influence of the Excise Act of 1745 was that of establishing glassmaking in Ireland. The industry had been in existence there since the end of the seventeenth century but its activities did not reach any artistic importance. As it happened, the Excise Act did not apply to Ireland, and this circumstance encouraged English glassmakers to bring their workmen into the country and there set up glasshouses where they could have a freedom of expression not now economically permissible in England. This freedom, however, was tempered by the fact that glass could not be exported from Ireland, and the glassmakers, therefore, were obliged to restrict their activities to the demands of the Irish market alone. This restriction was removed in 1780, thus giving glassmakers in Ireland full freedom to export.

Plate 35 ENGLISH CHINA
Opaque-white glass, enameled.
[*Victoria and Albert Museum photograph. Crown Copyright*]

Plate 36
A charming jug of Nailsea glass.
[*Victoria and Albert Museum photograph. Crown Copyright*]

Irish glass, therefore, was inspired by English ideas and was made by Englishmen using English methods, and it is hardly surprising that it reflects no national characteristics but is, indeed, indistinguishable from glass made in England. Among the English "settlers" was John Hill, who started work in a Waterford glasshouse owned by the brothers Penrose, whose name is sometimes to be found on the seal of genuine Waterford pieces. Hill brought with him between fifty and seventy workers skilled in all the branches of the industry, including cutting. He and his successor, Jonathon Gatchell, built up a business whose products had a world-wide reputation and gave to Irish glass of that period a claim to distinction.

Other works were established in Cork, Dublin, and Belfast, but the products of these do not differ from similar products made in England at the same time, so that it is difficult for collectors today to assign the origin of a piece with certainty. The Irish makers, however, have been helpful to this extent, that their pieces were sometimes stamped with a seal showing the maker's name.

Some Belfast glass has the name of Benjamin Edward, and Mulvany's glass, made in Dublin, has a seal bearing the letters "C. M. & Co." The existence of such a stamp settles doubt, of course, but when no stamp has been used, as is frequently the case, a disputed piece might just as well be of English origin for all one can say to the contrary. Less doubt, however, exists in the case of decanters, for these have shapes and a certain disposition of rings round the neck which are peculiar to Ireland and which, to the eye of an expert at any rate, help to identify their Irish origin with some degree of certainty.

Chapter Nine

JACOBITE GLASS

THE JACOBITE CAUSE

JACOBITE glasses give excitement even to the richest collection by their romantic association with a colorful and picturesque phase of British history; and to this excitement is added a spice of mystery sufficient to titillate the palate of the contentious or stimulate the appetite of the curious. Very often the glasses are nothing in themselves but are prized for their engraving, or rather for the substance of their engraving, for much of this work was done by amateurs whose work was not always good.

The value of Jacobite glasses, therefore, lies not so much in the workmanship as in the ideas that inspired that workmanship. It is the symbolism embodied in Jacobite designs wherein lies the main attraction of these glasses, for through that symbolism one is reminded of a loyalty to a cause which, however mistaken or misplaced it may seem today, still glows with the warmth of an unwavering devotion (*Plate 37*).

Within these secret signs is the story of bold deeds and stirring events intertwined with the melancholy tale of hatreds and ancient wrongs that will never now be set right. The glasses themselves were used by many a rebel club or secret society to pledge the "King across the water" and to drink confusion to the Hanoverian Government and its "Wee, wee German lairdie," and because of these associations they have a glamor which even the unimaginative or prosaic find difficult to resist.

And that is the outstanding thing about this epoch; it can

never be considered with indifference, for those who study the '45 Rebellion, and the events leading up to it, end either by admiring the Jacobites or detesting them. To read this story of rash endeavor and loyalty to a hopeless cause and to remain unmoved is not humanly possible. Even those who see in the event nothing more than a piece of political incompetence cannot withhold their admiration for the spacious generosity and noble gallantry that distinguish the followers of Bonnie Prince Charlie. To admire is to be carried away on a surge of poetic emotion in which, by contrast, the solid qualities of the opposing faction seem commonplace and mean. Like the Devil, the Jacobites had all the good tunes, while the Whigs had nothing but unlovable virtues; yet, in spite of the overwhelming force of these rich, colorful qualities, there remains in the mind a hard core of common sense that resists the imaginative onslaught.

It is as if the heart and the feelings side with the Jacobites and the intellect with their enemies. Such a contest provided R. L. Stevenson with the material for the tense drama of his superb tale *The Master of Ballantrae*, and inspired, too, a host of poets and writers; but it should be noted that the battle is not always fought between two opposing factions, or even between two different individuals, but is waged within the single man, fought out within the selfsame breast.

From a common-sense point of view the Jacobite cause was never anything but hopeless, but it is the sheer hopelessness, the magnificence of the failure, that appeals so warmly to the imagination. The main difficulty was that the Jacobites had too many friends whose friendship was based not on any sense of loyalty but on the hope that it would further private causes of their own.

There was Louis XV of France, for instance, who delighted in any opposition to Protestant and Hanoverian aims provided it did not cost very much. Although his pleasure in the discomfiture of his enemies was genuine, and, therefore, flattering to the Jacobites concerned, he was not willing, and, indeed, had no intention, of giving their cause any real support. He was the kind of friend who prefers giving advice rather than practical assistance, but, in justice to him, it should be remembered that his advice was not always taken and that things might have been better if it had.

The friendship of the Irish, too, was misleading, for the Irish were out to further the cause of the Pope and so were not actuated

Plate 37

Tumbler engraved with portrait of the Young Pretender, surrounded by the legend "Everso Missus Succurrere Sec(u)lo C.P.R." Above is the royal crown and the words "Long Live P. C." and, below, the date "1745." Height $3\frac{3}{4}$ inches. [*The Royal Scottish Museum, Edinburgh*]

by a love for the Stuarts but by a hatred of Protestants, particularly when the Protestants happened to be Englishmen.

One would expect that the English Catholics might have been a little more steadfast than they turned out to be, but for all their secret societies and toast drinking, for all the energy with which they entered into treasonable plots, they knew in their hearts that the cause they espoused was not really a popular one nor one that could count on any reliable support. This knowledge did not diminish in any way the ardor of their feelings or restrict their love for playing the part of the rebel so long as these enthusiasms remained a nuisance rather than a threat to the Government, but it did seem to inhibit their valor when the time came for real action.

The main support for the Stuart cause was supposed to rest in Scotland, but that supposition was based on a misinterpretation of the facts. No doubt the Highlands was solidly behind the movement, but the Highlands is not Scotland, or even the most important part of that country. It was only a minority of the population who lived there, and, except for that minority, Scotsmen were strenuously opposed to Catholicism and, therefore, had no love of Jacobites. The few of their number who lent their support were those who felt that the way in which the Union of Parliaments had been engineered was a betrayal of their country, and they allowed their anger to overcome their religious convictions. Such gave their arms to further political aspirations of their own which were by no means compatible at every point with the Stuart cause, and in this way their allegiance was doubtful.

As for the Highlanders, they were not all as trustworthy as they are often represented to be. These men were little better than savages at that time. They lived in a feudal system, owing allegiance to their chieftain and to him alone. The chieftains themselves were unaccustomed to kingly authority, had never acknowledged it in the past, and had little intention of doing so in the future. They were all little kings themselves, set up on their own account, and their notorious jealousies and boastful family pride made it impossible for them to fit into any scheme for concerted action on a national scale.

What was left was a small band of loyal supporters. In them no king or cause ever enlisted more devoted adherents. Their sacrifices and sufferings commanded the admiration even of those who detested them most, and their memory will live forever in the hearts of all who recognize the highest qualities of nobility and human endeavor.

It is possible that this small, determined band might have won the day, but that is counting without the character of the principal actors. Neither the Old Pretender nor the Young had the skill to exploit for their own purposes the many different interests of their allies, neither had the grace to appreciate their true friends, and both were too easily swayed by the enthusiasms of badly informed agents. Thus was their cause hopeless before it started.

Now to say that the majority of Scotsmen were Presbyterian and therefore opposed to the Jacobites is to oversimplify the case. In any age it is only the few who feel political issues keenly enough to make great personal sacrifices; the rest are always indifferent. The '45 Rebellion was no exception. A few Scotsmen felt bound to organize resistance to the rebels, a fewer still felt called to fight on the other side, but the vast majority wanted nothing more than to live their quiet, uneventful lives, if only the few would let them alone and give them peace to do so.

Yet these homely people found the issue by no means clear cut, for they were often torn between two loyalties, being sentimentally for the Jacobites and intellectually for the Whigs. Usually it was the Whig side of their nature that won, for Whig principles were all on the side of common sense while the Jacobite appeal was mostly poetic. In the end the issue was not difficult to decide, for common sense, although dull, meant security and a settled way of life, while poetry meant discomfort and loss, to say nothing of dangers and risks.

But Scotsmen were not alone in feeling the pull of opposing loyalties. Many Englishmen experienced the same thing and, like the Scots, ended by taking the common-sense point of view. When Dr. Johnson, whose sympathies were for the Jacobites, accepted a pension from King George there was an uproar that seemed to affect everyone except the Sage himself, who bowed his head before the storm and let it pass, calmly wishing "the pension twice as large that they might make twice as much noise."

In defending himself against the attack made upon him at this time he confided to Boswell:

> Why, sir, it is a mighty foolish noise that they make. I have accepted of a pension as a reward which has been thought due to my

> literary merit; and now that I have this pension, I am the same man in every respect that I have ever been; I retain the same principles. It is true that I cannot now curse the House of Hanover; nor would it be decent for me to drink King James's health in the wine King George gives me the money to pay for. But, sir, I think that the pleasure of cursing the House of Hanover, and drinking King James's health, are amply overbalanced by three hundred pounds a year.

In this the Doctor gave expression to the feelings of many Englishmen at this time. After all, it would be an unusual political doctrine that could earn the sacrifice of bread and butter and self-interest from the ordinary citizen. Besides, the Stuarts had done much to antagonize their adherents. In Dr. Johnson's case his affection for their cause had already cooled long before a pension was mentioned, and it cannot be said that the pension was the price of his support. Boswell tells us:

> I have heard him declare, that if holding up his right hand would secure victory at Culloden to Prince Charles's army, he was not sure he would have held it up; so little confidence had he in the right claimed by the house of Stuart, and so fearful was he of the consequences of another revolution on the throne of Great Britain.

Nor was Dr. Johnson's diminished ardor exceptional, and it may be taken to indicate a change of mind experienced by many reflective men at that time. Even younger and less responsible men, rejoicing in the notoriety of belonging to a forbidden movement, had been undergoing a similar change although they were less aware of it.

It was all very well for a young fellow to defy convention and join a secret club, much in the same spirit as a son of a wealthy manufacturer might join the Communist Party today, and no doubt his toast drinking and intriguing were sincere enough, but when it came to the point, when it came to real action and real sacrifice, a hesitancy crept into his hitherto wholehearted acceptance of the Cause.

Arnold Fleming observes that these lusty young men, the hunting squires of England, were better at drawing corks than swords, but this is too sweeping a generalization to be entirely just, for, whatever faults they may have had, they certainly did not lack physical courage. The truth is, a change had taken place in their minds in spite of themselves which no amount of toasting or noisy professions of faith could alter.

It was an age of prosperity in which most of that class enjoyed advantages unknown to previous generations, and it becomes very difficult to rail against a government with much conviction when that government encourages all the factors that provide one's material advantages. The thing becomes a grumble because the petals in one's bed of roses are crushed; it is a complaint about nothing. But so long as no irrevocable decisions were being taken, it was all very romantic and picturesque and a good lark into the bargain.

Much of the ritual by which the conspirators were kept in a state of enthusiasm consisted of drinking toasts, nor was it necessary to meet privately to do so. "The King" might be proposed in a tavern, and glasses clinked over a bowl of water to signify to those in the know that the toast was given not to the reigning monarch but to the other "King across the water." Wineglasses were even supplied with a double bottom in which the lower part was filled with water so that one could keep on drinking to the "King across the water" all night and no one a penny the worse.

Then Lord Duff's toast was a great convenience in public places. This consisted of a simple code in which were used the initial letters of certain phrases. Thus one could drink to "T.U.V.W." without arousing the indignation of the Whigs present, for only one's confederates understood that the toast was "Truss up Vile Whigs."

SYMBOLISM OF THE ROSE

Jacobite glasses, because of their romantic association with the '45 Rebellion, and because the designs of their engraving are full of hidden meanings which, when revealed, can throw light on the character and habits of the times, have become of historical importance. They are highly prized by collectors, their popularity increases with the years and, in consequence, so does their price.

Recently W. Horridge has given a new theory to explain the significance of certain Jacobite designs and this has now the support of many eminent experts, but before discussing this theory it might be advisable to give an outline of the older Jacobite theories that have held the field for so long.

A common heraldic device used in Jacobite glasses is the rose (*Plate 38*). This consists of a rose that may have six, seven, or eight petals. In addition to the rose, the design includes a partly opened bud on the left and a smaller, closed bud on the right. One of the early theories holds that the rose stood for James II and that the larger opening bud symbolized James Francis Edward, the Old Pretender, while the smaller, closed bud represented Prince Charles Edward, the Young Pretender.

Another of the older theories took the rose to mean the Old Pretender, and the larger, opening bud and the smaller, closed bud stood for the Young Pretender and his younger brother, Prince Henry, Duke of Albany and York, respectively. Some glasses of later date show only one bud, and the removal of the other is explained by the fact that Prince Henry was appointed a cardinal of the Church of Rome in 1747 and was thus out of the running, being no longer an eligible candidate for the throne.

The single-bud glasses present certain difficulties however. E. Barrington Haynes, in *Glass*, points out that it is invariably the larger opening bud representing Prince Charles that is missing and not the smaller, closed bud representing Prince Henry. Another circumstance that refuses to fit obligingly into this theory is the existence of some single-bud glasses which are earlier than the two-bud glasses.

It may be, of course, that old glasses were engraved long after they had been made and that the date of the actual engraving coincides with Prince Henry's elevation to his cardinalate, although proof of this would be difficult. Then again two-bud glasses were being engraved long after Henry had become a cardinal. This could be accounted for by the operations of inexact engravers carelessly working from force of habit, but I doubt it. In any case one would imagine that, if the engravers were not particular, those who commissioned the work would be. Presumably the symbolism meant much to them and they were hardly likely to accept something that had ceased to have a topical meaning.

The objections to these earlier theories, therefore, are substantial and, indeed, make these theories untenable, so that when

W. Horridge advanced a new explanation that gave a reading of the symbolism more in keeping with the known facts, many doubtful people were grateful to him.

Horridge bases his theory on the assumption that the central rose does not represent either James II or the Old Pretender but that it is to be taken as signifying the triple crown of Britain, France, and Ireland. The large, opening bud is to be taken to represent Prince Charles Edward and the small, closed bud the Old Pretender.

Acting on the basis of this theory, but differing from it in certain particulars, E. Barrington Haynes, in *Glass*, renders the symbolism in the following way. The first glasses in which the symbolism was employed were single-bud glasses in which is shown the rose representing the English Crown and a single, closed bud on the sinister, or right, side representing the Old Pretender.

This device served for a few years, but when the Old Pretender's son, Prince Charles Edward, became fifteen, or, perhaps, when he reached his twenty-first birthday, he too was included and was represented in the place hitherto taken by his father and by the same closed bud, while the father was now shown on the senior or dexter side—that is, on the observer's left—by a larger, opening bud. From 1735, when Prince Charles was fifteen, or, perhaps, from 1741 when he reached his twenty-first birthday, the new device with the rose and two buds began, and it continued in that form until the death of the Old Pretender in 1766. This event demanded another change and the dexter bud was omitted, so that the design returned to the form of its first beginning.

The theory thus expressed gives a logical account of the development of the design which it may be found difficult to refute. It accounts for the fact that single-bud glasses came in before two-bud glasses, for the design started with a single bud, and it accounts for the existence of single-bud glasses subsequent to the two-bud glasses, for the design ended exactly where it began.

This theory, however, leaves out of account the Young Pretender's brother, Prince Henry—but what of it? Prince Henry never had a prominent place in Jacobite schemes, and if he was thought of at all it was as a kind of reserve player to be brought on to the field only in the event of certain eventualities that were always remote and would probably not come about in any case. His

a, *b*

c

JACOBITE GLASSES

a Bowl engraved with rose and two buds, thistle, oak leaf, and the word "FIAT"; foot engraved with Prince of Wales feathers. Mid-eighteenth century. Height $5\frac{3}{4}$ inches.

b Air twist stem; bowl engraved with rose and two buds, thistle, oak leaf, and star. Mid-eighteenth century. Height $6\frac{1}{2}$ inches.

c Air twist stem; bowl engraved with portrait of the Young Pretender within a wreath flanked by a thistle, rose with one bud, and a star. Mid-eighteenth century. Height $6\frac{1}{4}$ inches.

[*The Royal Scottish Museum, Edinburgh*]

Plate 39 JACOBITE "AMEN" GLASS

Engraved in diamond-point with the cypher "*IR*" and the figure "*8*," in allusion to James VIII of Scotland, and two verses of the Jacobite hymn. The foot is engraved in diamond-point with the words: "A Bumper" and "To the prosperity of the family of Lochiell." *Circa* 1750. Height 6½ inches.

[*The Royal Scottish Museum, Edinburgh*]

importance, therefore, was not sufficiently great to include him in emblematic representation.

In offering this explanation Haynes observes:

> Horridge thinks that on the two-bud Roses the larger bud always represented Charles; and the smaller one still represented James; and that such glasses were favored by the many Jacobites who considered that Charles, not James, was the real hope of the Cause. He further credits the equally common single-budded Roses to those who still regarded James as the rightful king. I have to dissent, partly because such a state of affairs suggests impolitic comparisons, if not differences, but chiefly because it offers no explanation of the numerous single-budded Rose glasses patently made after the death of James. If the larger bud represented Charles, how is it there are no late Rose glasses with that bud alone?

OTHER JACOBITE SYMBOLS

After the Jacobite defeat at Culloden the clubs and secret societies continued to flourish and another rebellion was planned to take place in 1750, if planned be not too misleading a term for preparations that consisted mainly of talk. The Government handled the situation with great wisdom, treasonable professions were allowed to pass unnoticed, until, in the absence of opposition, repeated protests began to pall, so that the movement was smothered at last in the boredom of its own making, and thus it died. Less is known about the activities of these clubs and their transactions than satisfies one's appetite for knowledge, but they have left behind them a memory of an epoch that was spirited and romantic, and some glasses whose graven messages might explain much if only we had the key to their mystery.

Among the rich symbolism of Jacobite glasses are sunflowers, the stricken oak, butterflies, grubs, bees and spiders' webs, and inscriptions appear such as *Fiat*, *Redeat*, *Audentior Ibo*, "Success to the Society" (that is, the Society of Jesus), and *Reverescit*. In Scotland a thistle took the place held by the rose in England and is supposed to represent the Scottish Crown. With this particular design, but with others too, a star is sometimes incorporated. It was the custom to pledge the toast with the star held outward and to touch it with the lips when the wine was being drunk.

In England the star was sometimes used with an oak leaf. The oak leaf may be taken to indicate the hope of another Restoration, although Horridge holds the view that the star and oak leaf have a direct personal reference to Charles II. In that case such glasses would be memorial glasses.

On the other hand, it would not be unreasonable to suppose that the oak-leaf design signifies the Boscobel Oak wherein Charles II found shelter. There is even a glass in which the engraving depicts the complete Boscobel Oak itself in which Charles's face can be discerned peeping through the leaves of the tree. The stricken oak, however, is in another category and probably stands for the House of Stuart in the dark days of its adversity.

Butterflies, daffodils, and forget-me-nots are other devices used to indicate mourning. There are, too, some Rose glasses showing a grub on the stem of the rose. Arnold Fleming thinks that the "grub gnawing away on the stem" means despondency for a lost cause, and he is not alone in holding this view. The theory is not a convincing one, however, for pictorial representation hardly goes so far as to depict the actual act of gnawing, and it is equally possible, for all one can say to the contrary, that the grub is just sitting, in which case it may stand for something else that is so far unexplained. In any case it is unusual for clubs or societies to concoct a device that will be used as a constant reminder to the members of their failure.

Among Jacobite glasses the Amen glass (*Plate 39*) is of first importance. Perhaps twenty of these exist, although a number of fakes found their way onto the market about 1930. Usually these glasses have a baluster stem with an enclosed tear, and there are some with an air twist stem. The engraving is done with a diamond point, and the design includes the initials of the Old Pretender, "J.R.8" (that is, James VIII of Scotland) and two or sometimes three verses of a Jacobite hymn which was to become the forerunner of the present British National Anthem. The hymn always ends with the word "Amen."

God save the King, I pray,
God bless the King, I pray,
God save the King.
Send him victorious,
Happy and glorious
Soon to reign over us
God save the King.

God save the Church, I pray,
And bless the Church, I pray,
Pure to remain.
Against all Heresie
And Whig's Hypocresie
Who strive Maliciouslie
Her to defame.

God bless the Subjects all
And save both great and small
In every station
That will bring hame our King,
Who hath best right to reign,
It is the only thing
Can save the Nation.
AMEN.

It was held at one time that Amen glasses were produced about 1720, but a later theory contends that although the glasses may have been made about that time the engraving is of a later date, not earlier than 1735 and, in some cases, even later than 1745. The engraving of all the glasses, however, is much alike, a circumstance that suggests that the work must have been done about the same time or, at any rate, within a limited period.

One of the important Amen glasses came from Dunvegan Castle, Skye, and bears the date 1747.[1] It is supposed that Amen glasses originated in Scotland, if, indeed, they were not all made there. Certainly the spelling of the word bless as *bliss* and the use of the Scottish title, James VIII, supports this view.

Jacobite glasses generally are not outstanding artistically and it is only a few that are remarkable in this way. To historians, however, they are not without value, and to all who possess a spark of poetry in their composition they have irresistible charm. A great number of the glasses were of Newcastle make, but the engraving, in which rests their main attraction, was done elsewhere, perhaps long after the glasses had been made.

Who were these engravers and where did they live? The question is never likely to have a complete answer, but we may guess that some of the work was done by amateurs. In cases where the

[1] The story of this particular glass is given in an article by E. A. Herraghty, "A Discovery at Dunvegan," published in *Scotland's S.M.T. Magazine*, December, 1942, p. 23.

work is fine one may trace the hand of a skilled craftsman, and these, likely enough, were silversmiths. But craftsmanship apart, the messages conveyed through the inscriptions and symbolism still retain the substance of mystery. Much yet remains to be discovered.

Specimens of Jacobite glasses are to be found in a great number of museums throughout Great Britain and in some in the United States. The collections in the Victoria and Albert Museum, London, the Royal Scottish Museum, Edinburgh, and the Corning Museum of Glass are outstanding in their range and variety.

Chapter Ten

VICTORIAN GLASS—MODERN DESIGN

ANGLO-IRISH GLASS

AS we have seen, the Excise Act of 1745, which was followed by further increases in the duty levied on glass empowered by Acts passed in 1777, 1781, and 1787, had a harmful effect on the craft in England. One of the effects of these increasing impositions was to encourage the making of glass in Ireland where the tax did not apply, but, as Ireland was not allowed to export, the benefit of freedom there was limited by local demand. However, in 1780 Ireland was given free trade, so that, with the rich market of England open to her, glassmaking in Ireland was given a great impetus.

Irish glass, however, was made by English glassmakers who had come from Stourbridge and Bristol, and these men naturally used traditional English methods and expressed English feeling, with the result that Irish glass has nothing of a peculiar, national quality about it. It is really indistinguishable from English glass, and the term Anglo-Irish rather than Irish might be a truer description.

Classical shapes and solidity are the outstanding characteristics of Anglo-Irish glass (*Plate 40*). Deep cutting of parallel and intersecting grooves produced "raised" diamonds and gave prismatic effects; and the kind of crisscross cutting called "hobnail" became popular. These massive shapes when not wholly covered with deep cutting had the addition of gadroons, wreaths, flutes, and the flourishes admired by the taste of the Regency period. In England, too, a little of this heavy work was also produced, and not only produced but sold in spite of its much higher price. The rising class of rich merchants who had made fortunes out of the Napoleonic wars made this possible, for price alone was no barrier to them. So long as a piece was solid and heavy enough to proclaim its owner's financial status they were satisfied. Nevertheless, the advantages given Ireland were much too great to be affected by the competition of English makers handicapped by a heavy tax, and Anglo-Irish glass held the field.

VICTORIAN STYLES

When the tax was repealed in 1845 English glassmakers came into their own, but they did so at a time when good taste was being engulfed in a tide of crude vulgarity. The aim of Victorian art was to express through one's possessions an idea of one's earning capacity, and if art contrived to convey an impression of an income much greater than it was in fact, art had then served its highest purpose. Hence the heaviness of Victorian design, the solidity and pretentiousness, and, inescapably, the repelling ugliness. But Victorian art was not something for which the English were alone responsible. Certainly the name is English and is derived from an English queen, but the thing itself occurred throughout the civilized world and, as we have seen, was a parallel phase to the *Biedermeierzeit* in Germany.[1]

Far be it from me to join the ranks of these boisterous writers who decry Victorian taste and manners for the mere wanton joy of making game of their ancestors. In any case the joke has been repeated more than once too often and it begins to pall. It was G. K. Chesterton who said that contemporary art critics do not seem to realize that our time is an age like any other age. They act as if it were the Day of Judgment.

If you happen to share the view of the advance guard and feel infinitely superior to your great-grandfather, I recommend a walk down the main street of any modern English or American town. Have a look at the furniture displayed in the garishly lit modern stores. Observe the tasteless designs made to appeal to badly instructed eyes, consider the poverty of the shoddy workmanship, think of the unsuitability of materials and the awful things that can be done with colored plastics and cheap chromium

[1] See page 81.

Plate 40 IRISH CUT GLASS
Salad bowl. Height $7\frac{1}{4}$ inches. *Circa* 1800.
[*The Royal Scottish Museum, Edinburgh*]

Plate 41 ENGLISH GLASS
A paperweight in crystallo-ceramie in the manner devised by Apsley Pellatt.
[*Victoria and Albert Museum photograph. Crown Copyright*]

plate. If after this experience you still think yourself a better man than your great-grandfather, have a look at a row of prefabricated houses. If that cannot cure you, you are in a graceless state.

It is in a spirit of humility, therefore, rather than of overweening pride that I approach the subject of Victorian art. That Victorian art had many obvious shortcomings will not be denied, but, while we rail against its faults, let us not forget that many of these faults still persist today and that we of this generation have less excuse for encouraging bad design and workmanship in so far that our opportunities of becoming better informed are far greater than were those available to ordinary people a hundred years ago.

The period was one of unprecedented prosperity and expansion in which art was caught in a tide of lavish abundance. Materials were misused, there was a craze for elaborate and senseless decoration, pretentious shapes, and a kind of arrogant ugliness that discarded good taste. Glass was no exception to a tendency that pervaded every aspect of art, and it may be that the restrictions of the previous hundred years had contributed to this state of affairs by having robbed glassmakers of their skill so that they had become less able and sensitive on the artistic side of their craft.

But even if that restriction had never existed and nothing of the glassmaker's skill been lost through lack of practice, it is doubtful if the result would have been in any way different. It was fashion that dictated the result—and who can withstand that? Only exceptional people can live outside their own time and remain unaffected by the ideas and trends that are in the air.

At this time the mass production of glass by mechanical pressing in molds, an invention which took place in America sometime in the 1820's, affected the art of glassmaking, sometimes with woeful results. The style in pressed glass passed through several stages. Initially, but for only a few years, this new technique slavishly imitated cut glass patterns. This was followed in the 1830–1850 period by the production of "lacy" glass having an overall background pattern of tiny stippled dots which reflected the light and produced a delightful and sparkling effect. Still later, and especially during the so-called "brilliant" era of cut glass, 1885–1910, so much mechanically pressed glass, or pressed glass blanks that were lightly and quickly cut ones, was produced in such direct imitation of the fine and expensive cut glass of the day that the latter went out of favor. As E. M. Elville observes in *English Tableglass*:

> Pressed glass at once found a ready market, but the Victorian snobbishness which nourished the imitation also ordained the eclipse of the real; expensively cut table and ornamental glass quickly lost its fashionable appeal when an almost exact replica of it could be seen in every suburban parlour.

Pressed glass, however, in its early stages is often outstanding for the quality of its metal. Later the technique was used for decoration other than the imitation of cut glass, and the designs made in low relief then became the forerunners of a modern style which, when it is properly understood and applied with restraint, can give most attractive results. Nor should such work be despised simply because the article is machine-made and cheap.

Cased glass—that is, clear glass which has been covered over or "cased" with a colored glass such as ruby, blue, or opaque white—became popular in the mid-nineteenth century. This was used by cutting away the top layer to form decorations in geometric designs which might appear transparent on a colored ground or colored on a transparent ground. Pictorial engraving and the engraving of flowers and foliage were also done in the manner of the Bohemian glassmakers, but never with a skill equal to that of the German craftsmen.[1] For all that, this work is not without an artistic merit of its own. Makers mainly in Stourbridge and in Newcastle specialized in this work, but the productions of a Birmingham firm, Bacchus & Son, are perhaps the most outstanding examples.

Mention should also be made of a new process called Crystallo-ceramie or Cameo Incrustation devised by Apsley Pellatt during the first quarter of the nineteenth century. This consisted of a cameo molded in a porcelain paste which was then enclosed in glass (*Plate 41*). Usually the designs took the form of classical heads or figures and sometimes of portraits of reigning monarchs. There is a flask in the Victoria and Albert Museum in which is embedded in the glass a portrait in relief of George IV, and many people are familiar with a glass paperweight in which is enclosed a cameo of Queen Victoria.

[1] See page 82.

Pellatt, by the way, was one of those energetic characters in which the nineteenth century abounded. He was a Member of Parliament, he acted on numerous committees and gave much of his time to the service of the public. Nor was this done to the neglect of his business, for his reputation as a manufacturer and authority on glass stood high. In the midst of his busy life he managed to travel a good deal and had time to write two books about his craft that won him fame. He also invented and patented a special mold for glassmaking. It was mainly through his influence that English glassmakers took to making copies of ancient designs.

These designs, which were modeled on the Egyptian or Grecian work of antiquity, were not prepossessing to say the least and we may believe that the first essays were deplorable. However, the phase coincided with the relief of the industry from excise duty, and the work was undertaken in a spirit of renewed energy in which a craze for ornamentation gained complete mastery over critical judgment until it became an offense to reason.

In six years of misguided progress a bewildering mass of bizarre forms was produced, and the culmination of all this exuberant enthusiasm was the exhibits of the glassmakers given to the Great Exhibition of 1851 that was held in the Crystal Palace. The Crystal Palace itself was made almost entirely of glass—nearly a million square feet of it—and what could be a more fitting temple for the worship of the glassmaker's skill?

The Great Exhibition was a big idea put over in a big way, and the glassmakers responded to this archetype of sheer size by producing immense chandeliers and fountains of cut glass. The whole thing was done in an overpowering way, every technical resource and contrivance of color were pressed into service, and the public, breathless with surprise, was thus enabled to see how magnificently glassmakers could rise to a great occasion.

Alas for human hopes! The mighty striving and devoted toil went for nothing, and all the overdone elaboration ended by bringing results far different from those intended. If the Crystal Palace proved anything, it was that artistic feeling was deficient in England, and it was from that date that the decline of English cut glass began.

But if glassmaking failed in the artistic field, it gained in the province of technology. Chief among the innovators producing better glass by more efficient means was R. L. Chance of Nailsea and Birmingham. Chance's activities were mainly directed to making glass for building and industrial uses, but his experiments in colored glass marked an advance that was not without important influences on the artistic side of the craft.

One of the consequences of the Crystal Palace Exhibition was to initiate a fashion for glass modeled on museum pieces, and this led inevitably to a phase of the art that lacked vitality. Work after the Bohemian manner in cased glass also became very popular, and remained so for many years as did an imitation of Syrian enameled glass made by lithographic transfer printing, which, if cheapness be a virtue, could at least claim to be that. It was an age of imitation and absurdity, but perhaps the most ludicrous results were reached when Victorian craftsmen turned to making glass in the baroque style of the Venetians. Here was the thing! Here was all the fuss and elaboration that appealed to a people who could admire fretwork and did not find dusting an objectionable occupation.

CUT GLASS

Cut glass continued in the Anglo-Irish manner, but declined quickly in popularity chiefly because cheap, machine-made imitations detracted from the value of genuine work. The production in quantities of a debased form of the art was enough to condemn it in the eyes of the fashionable world, although those who could understand and appreciate good craftsmanship for its own sake might still have been numerous enough to give sufficient encouragement. These latter, however, were influenced by Ruskin, who had a personal dislike of cut glass, and indeed hated it, so that, with the factories on the one hand throwing onto the market their daily output by the crateload, and Ruskin, on the other, calling down curses from Heaven, glass cutters had a poor time of it.

Ruskin's condemnation of cut glass possibly arose from his dislike of this form of decoration, and although few critics today would agree with his judgment, his criticism when applied to the overdone cutting then in vogue was perhaps richly deserved. Nevertheless, to dismiss all cut glass as bad because some of it is so, is to place one's self in a position that can hardly be sustained, and we may consider Ruskin's views as being biased and arising from personal prejudice and a misunderstanding of the real character of glass. Of this character he writes in Appendix 12 of *The Stones of Venice*:

> These are two, namely, its DUCTILITY when heated, and TRANSPARENCY when cold, both nearly perfect. In its employment for vessels, we ought always to exhibit its ductility, and in its employment for windows its transparency. All work in glass is bad which does not, in a loud voice, proclaim one or other of these great qualities.
>
> Consequently, *all cut glass* is barbarous: for the cutting conceals its ductility, and confuses it with crystal. Also, all very neat, finished, and perfect form in glass is barbarous, for this fails in proclaiming another of its virtues, namely the ease with which its light substance can be moulded or blown into any form, so long as perfect accuracy be not required.

That criticism, however, leaves out of account another peculiarity in the character of glass, namely, that when glass has cooled it becomes as hard as rock. Therefore, transparency apart, glass has two qualities, not one, in that it is soft and ductile in a heated state but hard and brittle when it has cooled. In its heated state a plastic treatment is natural to it, but in its cold state when its character has changed from soft to hard, a glyptic treatment is no less natural. W. A. Thorpe in *A History of English and Irish Glass* points this out to us, and when he says that Ruskin entirely misunderstood the character of glass, few will be found to disagree.

Yet, for all that, there is much truth in Ruskin's accusation when cutting is applied indiscriminately, and the term barbarous applied to such cases is not inapposite. Apparently William Morris thought so, too, but Morris with his extensive knowledge of craftsmanship and his sensitive feeling for beauty set about making glass to conform to his own ideas, since glassmakers seemed incapable of providing what he required, so that, while the cut glass of the period only produced in Ruskin a hatred that found relief in the outpouring of destructive criticism, it spurred Morris to create something better.

Morris engaged an architect, William Webb, to design glasses that would embody the principles of form and decoration he thought proper to the medium, with the result that a new conception of glass arose which was to have great influence on English craftsmanship. You are not to suppose, however, that the superiority of the new style was at once apparent to everyone and that people suddenly lost a taste for showy and meretricious designs simply because better things were being made available to them. On the contrary, the new movement gathered impetus only by slow and imperceptible degrees; but it persisted and grew into that nobility and purity of form which is the highest achievement of the best in English glassmaking at the present time.

Morris's glass was made by James Powell & Sons at the Whitefriars Glass Works in London, and there can be little doubt that in giving practical effect to the requirements laid down by Morris much, if not everything, was due to the genius of H. J. Powell himself. Powell shared Ruskin's view of cut glass up to a point, but was not persuaded that because some cut glass was barbarous it was all so. Cutting he thought legitimate when applied with the restraint practiced in the Roman periods by craftsmen who understood so well the real value of this form of decoration when kept in its proper place, and done in such a way that it enhanced and brought out the qualities given the vessel by the breath of the glass blower.

"Cutting," he writes, "applied in such a way as to proclaim the brilliance of glass, without obscuring or cloaking the form given by the glass blower's breath, helps to illustrate an essential quality of material and should no longer be regarded as barbarous."

The new style initiated by Morris and given effect by Powell was the beginning of the modern phase of the art which is today producing work of originality and aesthetic appeal (*Plate 42*). Whitefriars Works, which has kept in the van of the movement, has produced designs by Barnaby Powell, James Hogan, and Tom Hill which may be classed among the highest achievements of the modern glassmaker. And in this, skill and good taste in the glass blower's manipulation is combined with excellence of metal, whether colored or clear or tinted with smoky hues of brown or black.

Part of the new tradition lies in wavy surfaces and in having the sides of the vessels made in varying thicknesses which, acting as a lens, holds the play of light, thereby giving brilliance and that charm that is the peculiar quality of glass (*Plate 43*). Engraving and cutting, as these arts are now employed, are restrained and subtle in effect. Shallow faceting and simple lines characterize

'*late* 42 MODERN CUT GLASS

ʌ fine example of modern cut glass in which the art of cutting fits the art of glass ·lowing as aptly as music blends with words in an immortal song. Here neither raftsman has endeavored to eclipse the other, but both are in harmony, the one omplementary to the other, each adding something to a perfect whole. This ·iece was made by James Powell & Son of Whitefriars Glass Works.

Plate 43 MODERN ENGLISH GLASS

Two vases made by James Powell & Son of Whitefriars Glass Works which illustrate traditional influences on modern glass. In these a grand simplicity has been maintained which shows how the glassmaker, by adapting old ideas to modern needs, not only preserves tradition, but gives something of his own in the process to create a new phase.

cutting done in the modern style; and engraving by the wheel, by suffering the exercise of restraint, has broken the trammels of past traditions to reach new regions of greater expression and wider possibilities.

Other makers contributing to the modern tradition are Stuarts, Thomas Webb & Son, and Webb & Corbett, all of Stourbridge, and Walsh Walsh & Co. of Birmingham; and among the designers of engraving Graham Sutherland, Eric Ravilious, and Clyne Farquharson are outstanding.

In Scotland the Monart Works in Perth has given to the application of enamels a modern interpretation that is full of interest. Monart design is based on those simple shapes of hand-made pottery that are so admirably suited for vases used for holding flowers. The coloring of the glass fits well with the pastel shades of modern house decoration, and ranges from delicate pinks and blues to living greens and flaming reds.

Applying color to the glass is a tricky business. A small gathering on the end of the blowpipe is blown first of all. This is dipped again and blown once more, until in the repetition of this process the sphere at the end of the blowpipe is a mass weighing as much as twenty pounds or even more. The enamels are added at the various stages throughout the formative stages of the vessel, so that attractive effects in harmonizing or contrasting colors are obtained.

Blending different colors of enamel calls for skill and experience, for some colors blend easily, others are the reverse. Luster effects are obtained by applying gas fumes, and in this, as in the blending of color, it is hardly possible to get results that are exactly similar each time. That circumstance, however, gives Monart glass an individual quality that adds both to its value and attractiveness.

Engraving in Scotland lost popularity towards the first quarter of the present century, and within the last ten or twelve years the imposition of a purchase tax finally brought its practice to an end, at least so far as commercial production was concerned. In recent years, however, this art has been resuscitated by a small group of freelance engravers, three of whom have given an outstanding contribution to the art of glass decoration.

The first of these is Helen Monro, wife of the late Professor W. E. S. Turner, the eminent glass technologist, and it would be true to say that the present revival of the art in Scotland owes its existence to her. She is a sensitive artist and a craftsman of superb skill whose gifts have been enriched and given depth by a painstaking scholarship. Her engraving of figures has a certain kinship with the best of the Swedish art that has come from Orrefors, but it also contains much of Helen Monro's own originality (*Plate 44*).

Alison Geissler and Harold Gordon follow in the path opened by Helen Monro. Both are craftsmen of more than ordinary ability, and both bring to the art the invigoration of fresh minds. Indeed, although Scotland has known periods when many engravers found employment, none in the past ever reached anything near to the high level occupied by the present exponents of the art. How fortunate that at the very time engraving in Scotland should appear to be under an eclipse the art should suddenly soar upwards into the high noonday of its highest achievement.

Mention should be made here of the factory glass made by Stevens & Williams of Stourbridge. The products of this maker were designed by an architect, Keith Murray. Being machine-made, the vases and tableware are designed externally and produced by blind mechanical repetition, but, even so, the designs have been conceived with such an understanding of material and process that they are worthy of inclusion in any collection. Some of Keith Murray's designs are included, very properly, in the collection of the Victoria and Albert Museum.

THE MODERN PHASE

Now it may seem that I wander from the point when I mention the work of living artists here, in that the collector's interest is centered in the masterpieces of the past. There is another point of view worth considering, however. Contemporary work cannot remain so for very long, and Time changes the Present into the Past. The collector, therefore, who includes in his collection some of the best specimens of his own time and who sees that such pieces are properly specified in his catalog may be doing a useful service to posterity, for which a generation two hundred years hence will have reason to be thankful.

There are other reasons to justify the inclusion of modern glass in a collection, for modern glass is the outcome of a development that has taken a hundred years to reach its present state and is not

Plate 44 MODERN WHEEL ENGRAVING
Simplicity, charm, and a wealth of feeling are brought out in this attractive piece, "Jane," done under the wheel by Helen Monro.

Plate 45 NORTHWOOD VASE
A fine example of John Northwood's engraving. The body of this vase is decorated with a frieze of equestrian figures taken from the frieze of the Parthenon, familiarly known as the "Elgin Marbles." The relief of the figures is as much as $\frac{1}{8}$ inch from the ground and the remainder of the surface of the base is decorated with ivy leaves, honeysuckle and arabesques. Height $15\frac{1}{2}$ inches. Compare with Plate 16. [*Birmingham City Museum and Art Gallery*]

yet come to the end of its possibilities. It is not something that suddenly came about to suit modern furniture and modern house decoration, although these things have no doubt had some influence upon it, and it should be seen as part of the pattern of history.

The different conception of glass initiated by Morris came at a time when current fashion was incompatible to it, and although in its beginnings it appealed to a few discerning people, it was so out of tune with prevailing moods and ideas that it seemed to the majority something freakish, a kind of Pre-Raphaelite Movement in Glass only of interest to cranks. Yet, in spite of the atmosphere of crushing discouragement of the times, it survived, persisted, and slowly waxed strong until it attained a position of first importance.

It did so because it was something more than mere imitation, because it was the embodiment of that vital spirit without which there can be no real or lasting advance. Nor was it something ephemeral, a novelty to catch the fancy of a moment, but, as it was to be proved, something genuine and lasting. What these artists did, in fact, was not to invent something new, but, on the contrary, to take something that was old and adapt it to modern ideas and feeling, adding to it, at the same time, something of their own.

The modern phase, however, was not the only influence that arose in the nineteenth century. The Northwood School, for example, was of considerable importance. Unlike the modern school that gave a new interpretation to old ideas, the Northwood School adopted a close and faithful imitation of the great works of antiquity and for that reason its influence was restricted.

True, it brought to its task a superb craftsmanship, but although its followers were not less skilled as craftsmen than any others the movement did not survive and the modern movement did, because craftsmanship alone is not enough and can never make up for lack of a vital, creative spirit.

The founder of the Northwood School, John Northwood, turned from the geometric patterns of cut glass, then so popular, to produce relief carving on classical lines. The Portland Vase[1] was one of his models, and in making a reproduction of this he was

[1] See page 22.

occupied for over twenty years in experiment and trial before he succeeded. The actual work spent on the successful reproduction took three years of close concentration.

The technique required the cutting away of the outer layer of cased glass to show sculptured figures against a background of contrasting color, but, to achieve it, Northwood broke away from traditional methods by using an acid to remove the first layer and thereafter carving with hand tools and occasionally using an engraver's lathe.

Another piece of importance made by him is a Grecian vase ornamented with the Elgin Frieze of Horsemen (*Plate 45*). The tradition thus begun was carried on by his son, and soon attracted to itself a number of highly skilled craftsmen among whom George Woodall, Alphonse Lechevral, J. M. O'Fallan, J. Hodgetts, and B. Fenn are the most outstanding. These formed the Northwood School and were notable for the excellence of their craftsmanship and their ambition to break away from the vain repetitions of geometric designs to create something of real worth.

But the School survived only until the beginning of this century, yet, short as its existence was, it has left behind a reputation of a high endeavor that was little short of perfection and a number of specimens now greatly prized by collectors not only for their monetary worth, but for the aesthetic pleasure such rare pieces are able to confer.

Plate 46 NETHERLANDISH GLASS IN VENETIAN STYLE
In this wineglass, made in the late sixteenth century, the Venetian manner has been adapted in Netherlandish taste for stateliness and dignity.

[*Victoria and Albert Museum photograph. Crown Copyright*]

Plate 47 NETHERLANDISH GLASS IN VENETIAN STYLE
Both these wineglasses are typical of Netherlandish glass in the Venetian manner and both were made about the middle of the seventeenth century.

[*Victoria and Albert Museum photograph. Crown Copyright*]

Chapter Eleven

DUTCH, FRENCH, AND SWEDISH GLASS

DUTCH GLASS

THE early glass of the Low Countries is in no way different from the *Waldglas* common to Teutonic civilization and it was not until the Dutch had thrown off the Spanish yoke in 1609 that glassmaking became a vigorous industry in Holland. Many new glasshouses were set up at that time, and the craft throughout the Netherlands was in the hands of Venetian or Altarist workers.

Later the influence of English and German styles began to have an effect, in that Italian styles were adapted to the Dutch and Flemish feeling for stateliness (*Plate 46*), but the change did not bring any form that could be said to be distinctly original (*Plate 47*). Towards the end of the seventeenth century Dutch glassmakers were engaged in trying to find a heavier glass to take the place of Venetian *cristallo* and in this they followed English technique although they did not use lead. As with German and English experiments directed in the same search, the Dutch glass of this period shows signs of crizzelling. No advance comparable to English flint glass took place, however.

It is in the realm of decoration that the Netherlands has given its finest contribution to glassmaking, and in diamond point and diamond stipple engraving Dutch artists are unsurpassed (*Plates 49* and *50*). Much of their finest engraving was done on glasses made in England, although it may be that some of these glasses were of Dutch origin and were copies of Newcastle products.

Towards the middle of the seventeenth century Anna Roemers

Visscher created an original style of engraving in which designs of flowers and fruit were supported by calligraphic flourishes executed with graceful ease. Her manner was followed by several amateurs who produced work of distinction, among these being Willem Jacobsz van Heemskerk. He was a cloth merchant, who found time to write poetry and plays besides doing glass engraving.

Following this style came a new method of diamond-point engraving which, by means of shading rather than by line drawing, imitated the effects obtained by German wheel engraving. This technique lent itself to portrait and figure drawing and a more sophisticated treatment. The "Royal Oak" goblet, the "Scudamore Flute" and other English pieces of the period attributed to the workers of the Duke of Buckingham are engraved in this way.[1]

It is possible that these famous English glasses may be of Dutch origin, or that they were made in England and engraved in Holland. It is equally possible that they were made in the Duke of Buckingham's works and engraved by a Dutchman living in London. While there is no certainty about the place of origin of such pieces, or whether the engraving was done in England or Holland, it is generally agreed that the actual engraving is the work of a Dutch artist.

In the eighteenth century, wheel engraving was introduced into Holland and superseded diamond-point engraving for a while. This art was brought from Germany and was practiced first by Germans who had come to live in Holland (*Plate 49*). One of the most distinguished of these was S. Jacob Sang, who may have been a son of A. F. Sang, a Thuringian engraver.

A renewed interest was taken in diamond-point engraving in the eighteenth century when Frans Greenwood[2] devised a new technique which gave delicate and attractive results. Greenwood used a hammer and, by tapping the handle which held the diamond, produced stippled effects (*Plate 50*). While Anna Roemers Visscher had used stippling to achieve some of her effects, Greenwood relied on stippling alone. Such was his skill that he has given to this style a transient beauty and charm that is all its own. Greenwood is an English name, and it is likely

[1] See page 64.
[2] See page 90.

Plate 48 DUTCH ENGRAVING
A Newcastle wedding goblet, engraved probably at Amsterdam, with a Dutch coat of arms and dated 1740.
[*The Royal Scottish Museum, Edinburgh*]

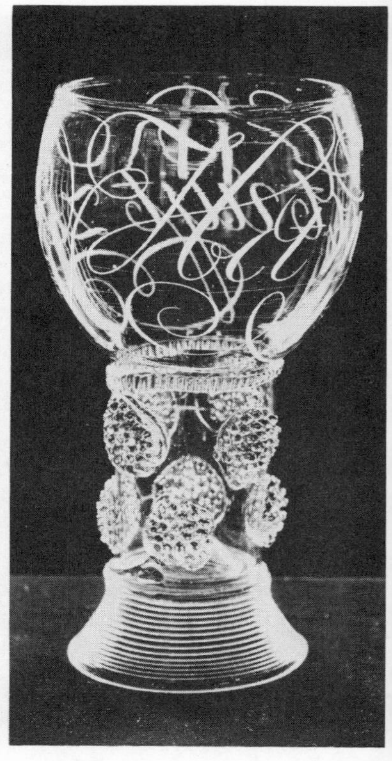

Plate 49 DIAMOND ENGRAVED DUTCH GLASS
These two *Römers* are of Dutch make and are good examples of Dutch diamond engraving. [*Victoria and Albert Museum photograph. Crown Copyright*]

enough that he was the descendant of an Englishman who had settled in Holland.

In the last forty years of the eighteenth century stippling by diamond point had a considerable vogue and among the most outstanding engravers of that time was David Wolff. Indeed, Wolff has given his name to this style of decoration, which is often loosely called Wolff, whether the work was done by him or not.

By the nineteenth century Andries Melort was engraving with a diamond point using line and stippling. His work was not applied to vessels, but was done for its own sake. He copied onto flat glass sheets pictures by various Dutch artists. The nineteenth century also saw a revival of stippling after the Wolff manner, and, in more recent times, this work has been carried out by E. Voet and other Dutch artists.

Mention should be made here of Zeuner, who engraved silver or gold leaf laid on the underside of glass in the manner known as *églomisé*. The word *églomisé* is derived from Glomy, a Frenchman, who first employed this process, which consists of applying silver or gold leaf to the undersurface of glass. This was then engraved by scratching with a pointed tool, and, when that had been done, a layer of varnish or tin foil was placed over the surface to protect it. Zeuner, who lived in the eighteenth century, did a number of large panels with pictures of English scenes.

FRENCH GLASS

The work of the French stained-glass artists of the twelfth century remains unsurpassed by any succeeding generation and may never again be equaled by the skill of man. For this success the artists working in glass at that time depended to a great extent on the richness of the colored glass available to them, and this was provided in the form of crown glass made by the Normans, and in broad glass made by the Lorrainers, in a quality of color of the highest rank.

The glassmakers then were kept busy, for much glass was required by the cathedral builders at home, but the production more than kept pace with local demand, and great quantities were exported abroad, particularly to England. Compared with English glass at that time, the French product was immensely superior. Conditions of transport, however, made English church builders long to have glass of an equal quality made at home, and their repeated requests to the authorities in France to send them glassmakers resulted in Laurence *Vitrearius* coming to England in the thirteenth century and so establishing proper glassmaking there.[1]

As we have seen, the development of the craft in England from that time was one of progress and increasing power. It is curious, therefore, that a similar development should not occur in France, particularly when one considers the understanding French glassmakers had of color technology, but the truth is that, stained glass apart, the craft did not outgrow the making of crude domestic glass in the Roman tradition, using for the purpose the primitive green *verre de fougère*.

As in the rest of Europe, Italian workmen settled in France during the Renaissance, but never for long in any one place, so that there were no glassmaking centers in France comparable to London, Stourbridge, and Newcastle in England. Glassmaking at Nevers, however, was an exception, and here Venetian and Altarist glassmakers and their successors settled for long enough to establish a tradition. The glass made there was in the Italian style, but, in addition, Nevers became renowned for the frivolous activity of producing toys and whimsies made of glass.

In Paris, Rouen, and other places the making of *cristallo* was in Italian hands and was a closely guarded secret in which native workers were given no chance to participate. So far as glass for ordinary use was concerned, the making of this was undistinguished and still in the Roman tradition and made of *verre de fougère*.

Even until the middle of the eighteenth century France lagged behind the rest of Europe and, being unable to supply her own needs, imported great quantities of glass from England and Germany. French ingenuity and originality apparently did not express itself through the medium of glass, but, in 1760, a prize offered by the Académie des Sciences for suggestions to improve the industry resulted in an awakening and the establishment of a number of new glasshouses in which better things became possible.

Two exceptions should be made to the general indifference of Frenchmen to the craft. The first was the invention of plate glass

[1] See page 44.

Plate 50 DUTCH STIPPLE ENGRAVING
An English glass with stipple engraving by Frans Greenwood.
[*Victoria and Albert Museum photograph. Crown Copyright*]

Plate 51 FRENCH GLASS
In this vase, made by Emile Gallé about 1895, blended colors give a most attractive, cloudy effect.

[*Victoria and Albert Museum photograph. Crown Copyright*]

by Bernard Perrot towards the end of the seventeenth century, and in this invention alone France may be said to have given the craft a contribution of great usefulness to mankind. The second was the invention by Desprez of a method of enclosing a cameo within glass in the manner of crystallo-ceramie, later to be used by Aspley Pellatt in England.[1]

In the nineteenth century, however, French artists were to devise new techniques of great originality that have had a considerable influence in the modern movement. Henri Cros rediscovered the technique of *pâté de verre*, used by the Egyptians for making vessels, masks, and amulets. *Pâté de verre*, or glass paste, is made by filling molds with powdered glass or frit of various colors and subjecting the molds to heat until fusion takes place.

Henri Cros and his son Jean used this method to make fairly large panels in relief, and in these the blending of color gave the work distinction. Later, in the beginning of this century, François Décorchement took the style a stage further in the modeling of bowls and vases in which the designs of birds and other forms were done in low relief. The soft, misty colors that blend so harmoniously with the pastel shades of modern house decoration give to this work a very strong appeal, but, apart from that, Décorchemont brought an original conception of glass that is not without an influence on the best work done today.

The second half of the nineteenth century is notable for the development of design in original ways. Joseph Brocard, Emile Gallé, and Eugène Rousseau opened the way to a new conception of glass that held wide possibilities. To some extent the work of these artists was influenced by Japanese art which was then creating great interest, for Japan had only recently been opened to the West.

Gallé in particular broke away from classical ideals and perfection of material to express himself in a way less restricted. He used colors blended to give cloudy effects, produced a wide variety of surface treatments including enameling and employed cased glass, which he treated with acid and engraved on the wheel to carry out his designs. Gallé's work is subtle, and he has given an interpretation of glass the possibilities of which, even today, are not yet fully exploited (*Plate 51*).

[1] See pages 112–113.

Thus, although France neglected glassmaking at the time when England and Germany were passing through a phase of great vigor, she has retrieved some of the lost years by the invigorating originality of her later artists through whom the work of the present time has gained something worthwhile. And it may be that the forward outlook inherent in the new French tradition is yet to result in greater things in the future.

SWEDISH GLASS

Another country that was influenced by the French artist, Emile Gallé, was Sweden. In the past the glass made in Sweden was undistinguished and the craft was not practiced extensively there or with the vigor that marked its advance in Germany and England. In Orrefors, in southern Sweden, however, a glasshouse was established in 1915 and from that time Sweden has produced work of the highest artistic worth.

Two Swedish artists, Simon Gate and Edward Hald, were particularly successful in engraving. Their work has a light touch and a subtlety that weds the engraver's art to that of the glassmaker, and it has about it an essence essentially modern that is most attractive. Then, in recent times, Viktor Lindstrand has produced engraving that displays a superb mastery and has the grace of fitting aptly to the material and form given by the technologist and glass blower.

Thus, although France and Sweden failed to participate in the art in the great phases of the past, these countries have made up for their neglect by the work of their immediate past and contemporary craftsmen. In doing so they have opened the way to styles not hitherto known to be inherent in this medium. That in particular is the triumph achieved by Emile Gallé, who, it may be, little suspected that the fresh attitude he brought to the subject was to have results so far reaching.

Chapter Twelve

AMERICAN GLASS

THE BEGINNINGS

GLASSMAKING is generally considered to be, rightly or wrongly, America's first industry, and was begun here in the fall of 1608, when the London Company erected a glasshouse in Jamestown, Virginia. The glassworkers were eight Germans and Poles, the first of a large number of glassworkers to be brought from Europe during the next three centuries to help establish an American glass industry.

The purpose of the Jamestown venture was not to produce glass for the use of the Colonists, but to increase England's source of supply for glass. This was highly desirable, since it was before the discovery of the use of coal for heating glass furnaces, and England's supply of timber was being rapidly exhausted. Since all of the basic raw materials for the making of glass were present in the new world, the theory seemed logical and sound; experience proved it otherwise. Little is known of the results of this first attempt to make glass at Jamestown, except that it ended unsuccessfully in 1609, and little glass was produced. Archaeological excavations conducted by the National Park Service resulted in the reconstruction of the glasshouse in 1957, for the 350th anniversary of the founding of Jamestown, where demonstrations of glass blowing are to be seen.

A second attempt was made to establish a glass works in Jamestown in the fall of 1621. This time the workmen were Italians. It is known that the factory was intended to "make all manner of Beads and Glass," but, contrary to widespread belief, the few remaining records and archaeological evidence point to the fact that no glass beads were actually made at Jamestown, and probably little other glass, if any.

Glass, especially window glass and bottles, two basic necessities, came into demand in what is now America shortly after the first colonization. Despite this demand, importations were practically the sole source of all glass used here throughout the seventeenth and much of the eighteenth century, for less than a dozen glass factories were established here before the American Revolution. Even after the Revolutionary War, and well through the nineteenth century, a large part of the steadily growing demand for window glass and bottles, as well as for tablewares, lamps, looking glasses, and other glass articles was supplied by importations.

Several other attempts to establish glass factories in the seventeenth century are recorded. According to documentary evidence, an attempt was made to establish a bottle glass factory in Salem, Massachusetts, in 1641. Little is known of this effort; it may have continued in operation only until 1643, but possibly the works remained in business until 1661. In New Amsterdam, now New York City, Everett Duÿcking established a glasshouse about 1645, and may have been succeeded by Jacob Milyer in 1674. Another glasshouse was established there about 1654 by Johannes Smedes. The products of these factories are unknown, or unrecognized, but it is likely they produced bottles having a bulbous body and a long tapering neck, and undoubtedly some hollow wares.

THE SOUTH JERSEY TRADITION

The first successful glasshouse in America was established by Caspar Wistar in Alloywaystown in South Jersey in 1739. Wistar was a successful brass button manufacturer of Philadelphia who had emigrated from Germany some years before. Like many later glass factory operators and owners, he was not a practical glassmaker, but an entrepreneur with capital to invest and a desire to supply the demands for glass in this country from a domestic source, as well as to turn a profit.

Like others before and after him, Wistar imported his glassmakers; at first, four men from Rotterdam, as shown by an agreement dated December 7, 1738. They were Simon Kreismeir, Caspar Halter, John Martin Halter, and Johan William Wentzell.

Sugar bowl, free-blown of green bottle glass in a South Jersey glasshouse, about 1780.
[*The Corning Museum of Glass*]

Offhand pieces in the South Jersey tradition, made in window glasshouses of South Jersey in the first half of the nineteenth century.
[*The Corning Museum of Glass*]

Pitkin flask of olive green bottle glass, with broken-swirl design. Eastern United States, probably Connecticut, possibly the Pitkin glassworks at East Hartford; late eighteenth—early nineteenth century.
[*The Corning Museum of Glass*]

Mid-Western Pitkin flask of green glass and grandfather flask of brilliant amber glass with broken-swirl designs. Both date from the early nineteenth century. [*The Corning Museum of Glass*]

The agreement was that these men would share in the profits from the factory and that they were to teach only Wistar and those men whom he designated the art of glassmaking. Caspar Wistar later imported other skilled workers from Poland and Germany. He died in 1752, but the business was carried on by his son, Richard, until 1780.

Wistar's factory was primarily concerned with the production of window glass and bottles, but though these staples were his "bread and butter" wares, this factory, and all others that followed him in the making of these two basic glass necessities, produced a limited number of tablewares, primarily for the glassmakers' families and other local customers. These "offhand" tablewares and novelties are characterized by individuality, rather than conformity to commercial requirements. Made from bottle and window glass, they were utilitarian and bold in form—sometimes even rather crude—and were often adorned with applied decorations of the same glass in the form of threading, gadrooning, prunts, and bands of rigaree, and sometimes even with naïvely ornate chicken-shaped finials.

This type of glass, which later was also produced in the small glass factories of other parts of New Jersey, New England, and New York, is referred to today as *South Jersey type*, and the entire movement is termed the *South Jersey tradition.* Pitchers, sugar bowls, milk pans, preserve jars of all sorts and sizes, candlesticks, and such whimsies as witchballs, hats, and canes, are among the by-products made in this tradition between the years 1740 and about 1870 (*Plate 52*). The influence of glassmakers from Europe—especially from Germany and the Lowlands—can be readily noted in these products.

The origin of the South Jersey tradition, however, is even deeper than this, for it has its roots in the so-called *Waldglas* that was produced in the small glasshouses in the forests of Central Europe that continued to exist after the fall of the Roman Empire in the West. While forms changed over the years, the basic character of such pieces and the decorative idioms associated with them continued to exist with little change right down to the eighteenth and nineteenth centuries in Central Europe, and were transported, in part at least, to the new world.

Glassmaking continued to develop in South Jersey after the close of Wistar's factory in 1780. From 1781 to 1850 at least twenty-nine glass factories were established in New Jersey, and 165 throughout the country. Some of the workmen who manned these glasshouses were from Wistar's factory, or were descendants of men who had worked there; others were new immigrants from the Old World seeking to better their fortunes.

The South Jersey tradition gradually spread to New England and New York. All told, about sixty glasshouses were established in New England, thirty-six of these before 1840, only six of which were for the manufacture of fine tablewares. The others were primarily bottle and window glasshouses, all of which produced a number of offhand wares. Among the earliest of these New England glasshouses working in this tradition was that established in what was then East Hartford and is now Manchester, Connecticut, in 1783 by the Pitkin family. It is known that this glasshouse was still working in 1817, and tradition says that it operated until about 1830, when it closed for lack of fuel, a frequent cause of the closing of these small works. Several petitions to the Connecticut Assembly for the privilege of operating lotteries for the support of the glass works indicate they were forced to shut down at times during the 1780's and early 1790's because of the lack of skilled workmen—a problem which beset almost every American glass manufacturer. Among the pocket bottles or flasks produced in this glasshouse was a finely ribbed or swirled and vertically ribbed type which has come to be known today by the generic term *Pitkin Flask*. Such pocket bottles with this form of pattern-molded decoration were not exclusive to this factory, but because many of the examples found came from this area and the Pitkin factory was one of a few known to collectors in the 1920's when such glass first became popular, it was natural that this name should be applied to it. Among other factories producing the same kind of flasks were the nearby Glastenbury Glass works, the Coventry Glass Works in Coventry, Connecticut, and a bottle glasshouse in Keene, New Hampshire, established in 1815. Almost all of these flasks produced in the eastern glasshouses were of olive green or olive amber bottle glass, finely ribbed and of a flat, ovoid shape. Pitkin flasks were also made in a number of mid-western glasshouses, where the colors were somewhat more varied, and the shapes somewhat fatter and more rounded (*Plate 53*).

Most of the offhand wares made in the South Jersey tradition

a

b

c

Plate 54

a and *b* Goblet and candleholder of dark green bottle glass attributed to the Keene (Marlboro Street) glasshouse, Keene, New Hampshire, 1815–1850.

c Sugar bowl made at the Suncook Glass Works, a window glass factory, Suncook, New Hampshire, 1839–1850.

[*The Corning Museum of Glass*]

a

b

a Pitcher with applied lily-pad decoration, threading and crimped foot, free-blown of light aquamarine colored glass in a New York State window glass factory, 1835–1850.

b Sugar bowl with lily-pad decoration and chicken finial contains a silver half-dime in the knop of the stem dated 1829 and a similar coin dated 1835 in the knop on the cover. Both of these pieces are excellent examples of the highest development of the South Jersey tradition.

[*The Corning Museum of Glass*]

in New England glasshouses were also of olive green or olive amber bottle glass; a lesser number were made from window glass, which because of the thickness of these pieces, usually appears to have a slight sea-green or aquamarine color (*Plate 54*).

The development of the South Jersey tradition found its fullest expression in those offhand wares decorated with applied decoration referred to today as *lily pads*. There are several variations of this form of decoration, which may have occurred to some extent in South Jersey, and is known on a number of pieces from New England factories, but which reached its highest degree of development and perfection on those pieces produced in this style in New York State glasshouses. Since most of these houses were concerned with the production of window glass, most of these pieces occur in light green and aquamarine colored glass, and date from about 1835 through the 1850's (*Plate 55*).

STIEGEL AND THE STIEGEL TRADITION

Henry William Stiegel, self-styled "baron," is the second of three outstanding figures in the early development of American glass, and undoubtedly the most romantic figure in the history of the industry in this country. He was born in Cologne in 1729, and came to America in 1750, settling in Schaefferstown, near Lancaster, Pennsylvania, where many of his fellow countrymen had settled. He was an ironmonger by trade who married his employer's daughter, Elizabeth Huber, in 1752, and in 1758 assumed control of the iron works upon the death of his father-in-law. He was an energetic and industrious man and was quite successful in the iron business.

With profits from his iron furnaces he established, along with several partners, three glasshouses. The first was associated with his iron works at Elizabeth Furnace. It was opened in September, 1763, for the production of bottles and window glass. In November, 1765, he opened a factory in Manheim, a small town near Lancaster which he founded, where bottles, window glass, and some tablewares were produced. A second Manheim factory was opened in 1769, and it was here that the wide variety of flint glass and fine tablewares, including engraved and enameled glasses, were made. His enterprise failed in May 1774, when Stiegel was placed in debtors' prison.

It was Stiegel's intent to produce glass of the same type and quality as that being imported to fulfill the increasing demand for glass from a domestic source. To do so he imported a large number of workmen from both the Continent and England who were skilled in the techniques required to emulate the products with which he intended to compete: German and Lowland peasant glass and English tablewares and bottles. Since the output of his workers was closely controlled, the products from Stiegel's factory were less individual in character than those produced in the South Jersey tradition. The result of the influence of the Stiegel factory on later glassmaking as it moved westward was the creation of a style known today as the Stiegel tradition. This tradition embodies the use of pattern molding as a decorative technique.

Stiegel was so successful in imitating both the German and English glasswares of the day, that, with some few exceptions, it is impossible to distinguish between them today. Two of the pattern molded designs which have no counterparts in England or Europe, but which occur on some pocket bottles found largely in the Pennsylvania area, are the diamond-daisy and the daisy-in-hexagon patterns. These factors warrant the assumption that these patterns may be attributed to Stiegel, and were quite likely made in his second Manheim factory between 1769 and 1774 (*Plate 56*).

Stiegel undoubtedly produced pattern molded flasks and tablewares with other, more simple designs, some of them in colors such as deep blue and amethyst. Chain salts, which may refer to a simple diamond pattern, are listed in 1769 in one of Stiegel's ledgers still preserved in the Historical Society of Pennsylvania. Other items listed in this same ledger include sugar boxes with covers, cream jugs, vinegar cruets, smelling bottles, fine wineglasses, jelly glasses, "sillabub" glasses, common salts, molded quart decanters, quart, pint, half-pint, gill, and half-gill tumblers, as well as quart mugs and bowls, pint mugs and half-pint mugs, and cans. Plate 57 illustrates some glasses of this description, which are typical of the products of Stiegel's factory.

The production of enameled glassware was begun by Stiegel in 1772. These glasses were made to supply the local Pennsylvania German market, and closely imitated the same type of enameled peasant glass which these people had been accustomed to in their

Plate 56
Pocket bottle of amethyst colored glass pattern molded with a diamond daisy design. Attributed to Stiegel's Manheim glasshouse, 1769–1774. Height $5\frac{1}{8}$ inches. [*The Corning Museum of Glass*]

Plate 57

a

b

a Covered sugar bowl of deep blu glass with diamond patter molded design. Attributed to th Manheim glassworks of Henr William Stiegel, Manheim, Penn sylvania, 1769–1774.

b Quart decanter of colorless flin glass with typical Stiegel-typ engraving, probably made a Stiegel's glasshouse about 1770.

[*The Corning Museum of Glass*

homeland. Since quantities of enameled tumblers were made in Germany and throughout Central Europe, as well as here in America by Stiegel, it is difficult to attribute most such glasses to Stiegel with any degree of certainty. However, there are about a dozen enameled tumblers bearing English inscriptions with distinctly Germanic overtones in the use of the language, which may well have been made in Stiegel's factory. They bear the following inscriptions: "We too will be true" and "My love you like me do" (*Plate 58*).

JOHN FREDERICK AMELUNG'S NEW BREMEN GLASSMANUFACTORY

John Frederick Amelung was the third outstanding figure in American glassmaking of the eighteenth century. He too, like Wistar and Stiegel, was a German who had been convinced after meeting in Europe such Americans as Benjamin Franklin, John Adams, Thomas Barkely, and Benjamin Crockett of Baltimore, of the desirability of establishing an extensive glasshouse in America. Backed by German capital in the amount of £10,000, Amelung landed at Baltimore on August 31, 1784, with sixty-eight glassworkers and equipment to establish the glassmanufactory he envisioned.

He acquired 2,100 acres of land on either side of Bennett's Creek, near the Monocacy River about nine miles south of Frederick, Maryland. Here he erected a glasshouse and by February 1785 was offering both "window glass, and green and white hollow ware" to the public. By 1787, apparently the time when he published his pamphlet, *Remarks Regarding Manufactories*, he had "erected all the necessary buildings for the manufactory, as glass ovens for bottles, window and flint glass, and dwelling houses for 135 now living souls." He also built for his workers in the town he called New Bremen a community house and a German school, as well as a mansion house for himself, which still stands.

In addition to the more common necessities of window glass and bottles, Amelung manufactured a wide range of tablewares. He also produced a number of engraved presentation pieces which are the finest glasses produced in America in the eighteenth century. The quality and form of some of these pieces may be noted in Plate 59. The covered tumbler depicting the story of *Tobias and the Angel* was made as a tribute to Amelung's wife for their anniversary in 1788. The form of the glass and type of engraving in the wreath which surrounds the vignette of *Tobias and the Angel* is typical of that found on some two dozen or so presentation pieces now attributed to Amelung, who is the only known glassmaker of that period in America to have left us any inscribed and dated examples of his work. The inscription on this glass reads: "Happy is he who is blessed with Virtuous Children Carolina Lucia Amelung. 1788."

Several engraved goblets made by Amelung as presentation pieces have capacious ovoid bowls set on rather large hollow inverted baluster stems and high domed feet, which are characteristic of Germanic glasses of a style some twenty-five or fifty years earlier. Since it was Amelung's intention to supply glasses then popular in America, it is somewhat difficult to account for his use of this rather old-fashioned form. Amelung also produced a wide variety of simple tumblers, bowls, bottles, flasks, and the like for everyday utilitarian use. As yet we have no extensive knowledge of this production, but it is known that he, like Stiegel, produced a number of pattern molded wares, such as the flask and salt shown in Plate 60. The design on the flask is an all-over diamond pattern, while the salt, one of a variety of colored wares produced by Amelung, is pattern molded in a checkered diamond design.

Despite the fine quality of his wares, the energy with which he pursued his business, and the encouragement of well-known citizens, Amelung, after operating only eleven years, was forced to admit failure, and his plant was offered for sale in 1795. He had been beset by a number of troubles, not the least of which was an apathy on the part of American citizens, who most frequently preferred imported wares to domestic ones. Also contributing to his failure were the lack of protective tariffs, and a bad fire which his works suffered in 1790.

Several other glass factories were established in the late eighteenth century in Philadelphia, Boston, and Baltimore, but relatively little is yet known of their activities. A glasshouse established at Kensington, near Philadelphia, in 1769, continued to operate under various managements into the twentieth century. On February 27, 1775, the Philadelphia Glass Works, as

Plate 58
Tumbler of colorless glass enameled with brightly colored birds, flowers and the nscription: "My Love You Like Me Do." Attributed to Henry William Stiegel's glasshouse in Manheim, Pennsylvania, 1772–1774.
[*The Corning Museum of Glass*]

Plate 59
Blown and engraved glass made by John Frederick Amelung in his New Breme
Glassmanufactory, New Bremen, Maryland. The goblet, or pokal, is dated 1793
the covered tumbler, a present to Amelung's wife, 1788; the flask, 1792.
[*The Corning Museum of Glass*

late 60
attern molded pocket bottles and salt and an engraved goblet made at the
ew Bremen Glassmanufactory, 1785–1795. (The Melvin Billups Collection)
[*The Corning Museum of Glass*]

a

c

Plate 61

a Loving cup, undoubtedly made as a presentation piece, free-blown of colorless flint glass with a George III 1810 florin or two shilling piece in the knop of the stem. Possibly made at the New England Glass Company, 1820–1835. Height 10 inches.

b Whale oil or fluid-burning lamp with pressed base and blown, cut and engraved font. Second quarter of the nineteenth century. Height $9\frac{7}{8}$ inches.

c Salt, pressed of colorless lead, or flint, glass, bearing on the underside of the base the inscription: "N.E. Glass Company Boston." About 1830. Height $1\frac{15}{16}$ inches. [*The Corning Museum of Glass*] it was called, advertised in Dunlap's *Pennsylvania Packet* a wide variety of glass, including fine tablewares, lamps of various sorts, pocket bottles, phials, and tubes for thermometers. Unfortunately, the identity of these products is lost to us today.

The Boston Crown Glassmanufactory was established in Boston in 1787 for the purpose of manufacturing quality window glass by the crown glass method. It was not, however, until 1793, when additional German workmen skilled in this practice were brought to this country, that manufacturing activities really got underway. From that time until the failure of the company in 1827, the operations of this glasshouse were highly successful and its product became famed throughout this country. In 1802, it established a subsidiary, the Chelmsford Glass Works in Chelmsford, Massachusetts, for the production of broad, or sheet, glass by the cylinder glass process. In 1811, it extended its crown glassmaking facilities by erecting a second factory in South Boston.

The earliest manufacturer of flint glass in the New England area was Thomas Caines, an Englishman who had come to this country from Bristol, England, in 1811 to work for the Boston Crown Glassmanufactory. He persuaded this firm to build and lease to him a six-pot flint glass furnace. He began operating this furnace late in 1812 or early in 1813, and produced a wide variety of tablewares, lighting devices, and "philosophical glasses." Caines continued to operate on this basis until about 1820 or 1823, when he established in South Boston his own Phoenix Glass Works which continued to operate until 1870. In its later years, when it was operated by his son, the factory produced cut glass, pressed glass, and lamp chimneys. Little is known of the products of this factory in its early years, but a number of bowls, pitchers, decanters, and other tablewares of blown glass with an applied chain decoration can be definitely attributed to this works. It is quite possible that this factory also produced what is known today as blown-three-mold glass and "lacy" pressed glass, though as yet no examples of these types of glass have been specifically identified with this factory.

Among the most outstanding glass factories along the eastern seaboard was the New England Glass Company, established in East Cambridge, Massachusetts, in 1818 and operating there until 1888. This company produced a countless variety of all types of glasswares including pocket bottles, common tumblers, blown-three-mold glass, lacy pressed glass, pressed pattern glass, cut and engraved glassware of all types, and in later years, a number of attractive art glasses. Among its early products were also a number of outstanding free-blown wares of fine quality flint, or lead, glass (*Plate 61*). The Company operated with great success from its inception until the 1880's when it began to feel the effects of competition from factories in the mid-western area where coal and gas as fuel for the glass furnaces were readily available at lower costs. Finally, in 1888, Edward D. Libbey, then proprietor of the works, in response to a negative reply from the union to return to work, moved the factory to Toledo, Ohio, where he established the Libbey Glass Company, which is still active today.

In 1825, Deming Jarves, a well-known figure in American glassmaking who helped to establish no fewer than five glass companies, and who had been an agent for the New England Glass Company since 1818, established the Boston and Sandwich Glass Works in Sandwich on Cape Cod, Massachusetts. This company, too, continued in operation until 1888 when it also succumbed to strikes by the glassworkers. It produced wares very similar to those of the New England Glass Company, including, especially during the 1850–1870 period, a number of cased and cut glasswares influenced by Bohemian glass of this type. Of all its products, Sandwich is probably most popularly known for the early, lacy pressed glass attributed to it, which has even taken on the generic term "Sandwich" glass (*Plate 62*). Several attempts were made to reopen the factory after 1888, but all were unsuccessful.

A number of other glasshouses producing fine flint glass wares developed in the East in the early nineteenth century. Among them were the Union Flint Glass Works established in Kensington, near Philadelphia, in 1820 by some workers who had left the New England Glass Company; the Jersey Glass Company established by George Dummer and partners in Jersey City in 1824, and continuing in operation until the 1860's. Pressed glasswares were added to the production of the latter factory about 1827, two patents having been granted to members of this firm for improvements in this form of manufacturing glass. John Gilliland, who in the fall of 1822 withdrew from the New York Glass Works which he and John and Richard Fisher had established in 1820, established the Brooklyn Glass Works in 1823,

Pressed glass bowl attributed to the Boston and Sandwich Glass Company. About 1830. Note the close relationship of the design to that of the cut glass bowl on the right, made in Ireland about 1820. The bowl in the center is from the Roman Empire dating from the third–fourth century A.D., and shows the continuity of design elements through the centuries.
[*The Corning Museum of Glass*]

Lacy pressed glass bowl probably made at Sandwich, about 1830–1835. [*The Corning Museum of Glass*]

Plate 63
Cut glass dating from about 1830. The sugar bowl and tumbler are attributed t
a Mid-Western American glasshouse; the pitcher is from England or Irelan
The same design elements were popular in both areas, making it difficult toda
to identify the origin of many such pieces. [*The Corning Museum of Glas*

which continued in operation until 1868. All three of these men had formerly worked for the New England Glass Company. The two companies they established also produced a wide variety of flint glass, cut and molded flint glass tablewares, as well as pressed glass. The fine cut glasswares produced by all of these companies from about 1820 to 1840 closely resembled the Anglo-Irish cut glass of that time, and it is difficult today to distinguish them from one another (*Plate 63*).

As the development of America continued, it was only natural that glassmakers, too, should migrate to the west. Pittsburgh and the surrounding area of what is now Ohio and West Virginia became an early center for glassmaking, its location offering both an easy access to coal for fuel for the glass furnaces, and ample waterways for the distribution of the finished product. It was here in 1797 in the Pittsburgh Glass Works established by Major Isaac Craig and Colonel James O'Hara that coal was first used for fuel in an American glasshouse. This was a factor which sounded the death knell of many glasshouses in the eastern part of the country which had not yet even been conceived, for as wood for fuel grew scarcer and more costly the glasshouses of the East were to find it more and more difficult to compete successfully with the numerous glass factories which came to be established in the Pittsburgh, or Mid-Western area, as it is called.

In addition to the advantages of a nearby fuel supply and of a good waterway system for distribution, it was only natural that this area should develop as a glassmaking center to satisfy the needs of a rapidly growing western population for glass, which was difficult to transport across the Allegheny Mountains. Again, window glass and bottles were the two products most urgently needed; the first for the growing numbers of houses, the second as containers for cider, beer, and whiskey. The importance of the latter to the economy of the area in the late eighteenth and early nineteenth century may be judged by the fact that "what a bank bill was at Philadelphia or a shilling piece at Lancaster, that was whiskey in the towns and villages that lay along the banks of the Monongahela River."[1] All sorts of bottles, demijohns, and carboys were produced in the numerous factories that sprang up in this

[1] John Bach McMaster, *A History of the People of the United States* (New York, 1883-1913), II, 189, as quoted in Helen and George S. McKearin, *Two Hundred Years of American Blown Glass* (New York, 1950), p. 47, n. 139.

area, many of which were decorated with pattern molded designs (*Plate 64*). Numerous tablewares in the form of tumblers, pitchers, sugar bowls, and the like, were produced as by-products by many of these bottle glasshouses, and many of these, too, were pattern molded with vertically ribbed or swirled ribbed designs, or diamond patterns. The influence of the Stiegel tradition may be readily seen in these products, which are perhaps some of the most appealing pieces of American glass (*Plate 65*).

Of the fifty glasshouses established in Pennsylvania between 1763 and 1850, forty were in Pittsburgh. Of these fifty, fourteen were flint glassmanufactories, and the balance were for the manufacture of window glass and bottles. The Pittsburgh Flint Glassmanufactory established in 1807 by Benjamin Bakewell and Edward Ensel was the first in this area to produce fine flint glass tablewares as well as bottles, flasks, and window glass. About 1810 the firm added cut and engraved glasswares to their output for which they are justifiably noted today, as then. In 1825 the company received a reward for the best cut glass pair of decanters at the second exhibition of the Franklin Institute. Cut glass tumblers, some engraved, bearing sulphide profiles of Lafayette, Washington, Andrew Jackson, and De Witt Clinton, were made by this firm about 1824 (*Plate 66*).

Apparently a wide variety of pattern molded tablewares of both colorless and colored flint glass was produced by Bakewell's, as the firm is popularly called, as well as free-blown, multi-colored, cased, and pressed glasswares. The first United States patent of which we know for pressing glass by mechanical means was granted to John P. Bakewell of Bakewell and Bakewell on September 9, 1825. It was for "an improvement in making glass furniture knobs." The company doubtless produced vast quantities of pressed glass during the early lacy period, from the late 1820's to the early 1840's, or so, but only relatively few of these patterns can be definitely attributed to the factory.

Pillar molded glass—thick blown glass having broad ribs projecting boldly from its sides—was another product of the Mid-Western glasshouses producing tablewares during the 1835–1870 era, and undoubtedly much of this type of glass was produced by Bakewell's. This sturdy glass was well suited for hard service on the many steamboats plying various rivers of the area, and is frequently termed "steamboat glass" (*Plate 67*). The Bakewell

Plate 64
Pattern molded pocket flask and bottle from Mid-Western glasshouses, 1800–1835. The bottle is of brilliant amber colored glass, and because of its pattern, is frequently termed a "swirl" bottle.
[*The Corning Museum of Glass*]

a

Plate 65

a Footed bowl of pale green glass patterned in a 24-rib mold, lat eighteenth—early nineteenth century, Mid-Western, possibly made in th New Geneva Glass Works. Height 5⅜ inches.

b Pitcher and sugar bowl of brilliant light green glass, with expande diamond pattern molding. Mid-Western, probably made in the Ohio Zanesville Glass Works about 1816–1830. Height of sugar bowl wit cover, 6⅞ inches. [*The Corning Museum of Glass*

a, b

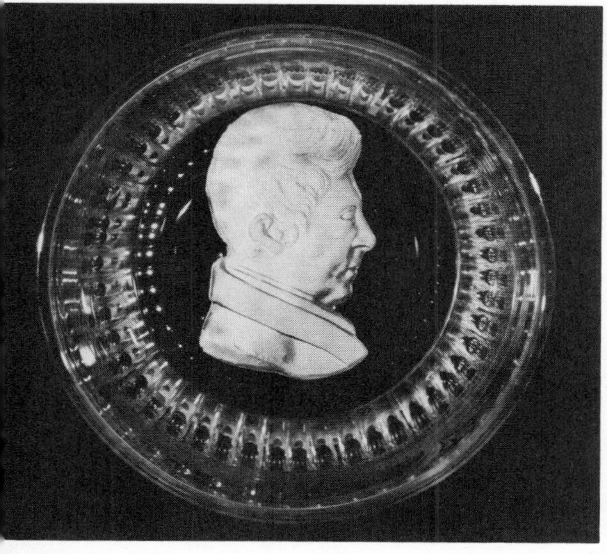

c

Plate 66

a Cut glass tumbler with a sulphide profile portrait bust of Washington in uniform in the base. Bakewell & Co., Pittsburgh, about 1824.

b Mug with cut glass pattern typical of both American and Anglo-Irish designs, 1815–1835, attributed to a Pittsburgh factory.

c Sulphide profile portrait of Lafayette in the base of a cut glass tumbler like that shown in *a*. [*The Corning Museum of Glass*]

Plate 67
Pillar molded amber vase attributed to a Pittsburgh or Mid-Western glasshouse, 1840–1860. Height 11 inches. [*The Corning Museum of Glass*]

Company continued in operation under various managements, but always with a member of the Bakewell family among the proprietors, until it closed in 1882. The quality of the company's products was world famous, and several presidents, including Madison and Jackson, ordered services of glassware from Bakewell's.

Among other glassmakers who migrated to the Mid-West was Charles Ihmsen, who had come from Germany in 1795 and started a factory in Baltimore in association with Amelung's son, Magnus. In 1810 Ihmsen moved to Pittsburgh and established the Birmingham Glass Works. Few products of this factory are known today, but the decanter shown on Plate 68 engraved with the famous naval battle of the War of 1812 between the *Hornet* and the *Peacock*, was made at Ihmsen's factory about 1813. It is one of the few pieces of American engraved glass depicting an historical scene.

Two methods which resulted in the mass production of glass and made it more widely available at greatly reduced cost were developed in America between about 1815 and 1830. The first of these was the reintroduction of the use of full-size molds of metal made in several parts which both formed the shape of the article and gave it its patterned decoration. This type of full-size mold came into use here about 1815, or a little earlier, and was used to produce what we call today pictorial or historical flasks of half-pint, pint, and quart size, as well as decanters and tablewares which are referred to today as blown-three-mold wares.

The pictorial flasks bear a wide variety of purely decorative elements such as sunbursts, urns, and cornucopias, as well as Masonic symbols, profiles of national heroes, presidential candidates, visiting dignitaries, and such patriotic symbols as the eagle and flag. In addition, the decoration on these bottles frequently commemorated some special occurrence, such as the coming of the railroads and the discovery of gold in Pike's Peak. These flasks were produced by many of the bottle glasshouses throughout the country, usually in colors of olive green, olive amber, and amber, but also in aquamarine and, more rarely, in brilliant hues of blue, emerald green, and amethyst. The forms of these flasks changed from period to period, and also varied somewhat within the same periods in different areas of the country (*Plate 69*). These pictorial flasks are a distinct American phenomenon in glass, having almost no counterparts in England or Europe.

Decanters and other blown-three-mold tablewares, which had become an important part of the production of American glass-houses by 1820, at first closely imitated Anglo-Irish cut glass, and indeed, were intended as a cheaper substitute for it. Among the earlier designs were simple combinations of vertical ribs and patterns of diamond diapering. A combination of these elements with varieties of "sunburst" designs appears to be the next stage in the development of patterns in blown-three-mold glass. These, in turn, seem to have been followed by designs unrelated to Anglo-Irish cut glass, but which may have been influenced by the interest in the Gothic revival. In addition, blown-three-mold designs developed somewhat more originally in patterns which are termed today "baroque" (*Plate 70*).

PRESSED GLASS

The invention of mechanical pressing of glass is credited to American glassmakers, and is a distinctive contribution to the art of glassmaking. The date of this invention is not precisely known. Small hand presses, much like pliers with especially designed jaws having a design cut into them, had been used in Holland, England, and Ireland, from about 1785, for the purpose of pressing stoppers for decanters and feet for salts. As mentioned earlier, the first patent of which we have knowledge for the mechanical pressing of glass was granted to John P. Bakewell of Bakewell and Bakewell and Company in Pittsburgh, on September 9, 1825. The second patent was issued to Henry Whitney and Enoch Robinson of the New England Glass Company on November 4, 1826, also for an improvement in the manufacture of glass furniture knobs. This was followed by a spate of other patents for various improvements in the rapidly developing technology of the pressing of glass.

Again, the very early pieces of pressed glass tended to imitate Anglo-Irish cut glass. Within a short time, however, distinctly American designs of lacy pressed glass were being made, probably beginning no later than 1830. The fine stippling in the background of these pieces which produced this lacy effect served a purpose other than decorative, in that the shear mark which

Plate 68
Decanter engraved with the naval engagement between the *Hornet* and the *Peacock*. Made at Charles Ihmsen's Birmingham Glass Works in Pittsburgh, about 1813. Height 11 inches. [*The Corning Museum of Glass*]

a

b

Plate 69

a Historical or pictorial flasks. Left to right: Shield and Clasped Hands, light blue glass, made by William Frank and Sons, Pittsburgh. Cobalt blue pint flask with Columbia on obverse, Eagle on reverse, probably made in Philadelphia in the 1820's. Olive amber half-pint flask with Eagle and Cornucopia designs, possibly made in East Hartford, Connecticut about 1815–1820. Emerald Eagle pint flask, probably made in Keene, New Hampshire about 1830. Light green Scroll flask, probably Mid-Western, 1830–1840.

b Left to right: Sunburst flask of colorless, lead glass, Keene, New Hampshire, 1815–1817; Jenny Lind calabash bottle, mid-nineteenth century; and a 2½-quart aquamarine colored flask probably made in the Louisville, Kentucky Glass Works. [*The Corning Museum of Glass*]

a Group of blown-three-mold glasses whose patterns are largely imitative of Anglo-Irish cut glass of about 1820.
[*The Corning Museum of Glass*]

b Blown - three - mold decanter with a baroque design, probably made at the Boston and Sandwich Glass Works, 1825–1835.
[*The Corning Museum of Glass*]

Plate 71

a

b

c

a Pitcher, lacy pressed glass, mad in the Pittsburgh, Pennsylvania Fort Pitt Glass Works of R. B Curling and Sons, probably be tween 1829–1832. Marked on th base "R.B. Curling & Sons For Pitt."

b Pressed glass boat salt, marked on the stern: "J. Robinson & Sons Pittsburgh." Made in their Stour bridge Flint Glass Works betwee 1829–1832.

c Pair of colorless glass candle holders with pressed lacy glas bases, combined with free-blown and manipulated sockets and stand ards. Made in a Mid-Wester glasshouse, probably in the 1830's

[*The Corning Museum of Glass*

remained in the glass even after it was pressed was hidden, and the dull, foggy effect which resulted on a plain surface by the contact of the mold upon the glass was almost unnoticeable. The rapidity with which the technology of pressing developed may be noted in the illustration of the pressed glass pitcher made in the Fort Pitt Glass Works of R. B. Curling & Sons, Pittsburgh, about 1830 (*Plate 71*). Those who are familiar with mechanical problems will recognize this rapid development when they observe that the handle is also pressed as a part of the pitcher, rather than having been applied by hand afterwards.

That the quality of this early lacy pressed glass was recognized then, as now, is evident from the comments of an English visitor, James Bordman, who was so favorably impressed by the glass exhibited at the Fair of the American Institute of the City of New York in 1829 that he included the following comment in his book, *America and the Americans*: "The most novel article was the pressed glass; which was far superior, both in design and execution to anything of the kind I have ever seen either in London or elsewhere. The merit of its invention is due to the Americans, and it is likely to prove one of great national importance." That this new method of producing glass was of great national importance cannot be denied, for the prosperity of numerous American glasshouses producing commercial wares during the next fifty to seventy-five years was based largely upon it. The lacy period probably ended, for the most part, in the late 1830's, though some such patterns, particularly in salts, continued through the 1840's, and was followed by simpler patterns which were eventually produced, in many instances, in complete tableware services, including creamers, pitchers, spooners, decanters, tumblers, goblets, and other forms (*Plate 72*). This pressed pattern glass was produced in glasshouses of both the East and Mid-West, and though most were of colorless glass, some patterns were also made in colored glasses. Such glasses are usually much sought after by collectors today, since they are usually much more rare than the colorless examples.

Numerous candlesticks, lamps, and vases were made of pressed glass. They were produced by pressing the foot, standard and socket, font or bowl separately, then joining the sections together by thin wafers of glass to form the complete piece. Thus, by combining different elements a fairly wide variety of articles could be manufactured with a limited number of molds. These variations provide an interesting challenge to the collector today (*Plate 73*).

ART GLASS

Enormous quantities of pressed glass continued to be made by American glass factories throughout the remainder of the nineteenth and on into the twentieth century, up until today. One should not lose sight of the fact, however, that as the production of pressed glass grew larger throughout the nineteenth century, blown glass continued to be made. Shortly after mid-century, a special interest developed in the making of colored glasswares and, beginning about the time of the Centennial Exposition in Philadelphia in 1876, in the production of objects whose forms and color effects often simulated materials other than glass. These "art glass" wares, as they were called then and now, vividly expressed the fondness for ornateness and colorfulness of the late Victorian era, and include such parti-colored or shaded glasses as Amberina, Peach Blow, and Burmese, as well as Satin Glass, Spangle Glass, Vasa Murrina, and, somewhat later, some decorated wares such as Crown Milano and Royal Flemish. The production of these wares was not restricted to America, but occurred simultaneously in many European and Continental glass factories as well. The production of art glass reached its apex in the 1880's and early 1890's (*Plate 74*).

Perhaps silvered glass, or mercury glass as it is sometimes called, may be considered as the first of these art glasses. One of the earliest patents for this form of decoration, whereby a solution of mercury was applied to the interior of a hollow blown vessel, was taken out by Hale Thomson of London. Varnish & Company of London produced a number of very handsome silvered glasswares using his process. In America, William Leighton of the New England Glass Company patented a means for producing silvered glasswares in January, 1855. Some of the finest examples of silver glass made in America were produced by this company, many of them being marked on the base by a metal disk bearing the initials "N. E. G. Co." underneath a colorless glass disk which tightly sealed the hole in the base of the article by means of which the mercury had been poured into the vessel. This tight

a Creamer, California pattern, made by the New England Glass Co., about 1870.
[*The Corning Museum of Glass*]

b Goblet, New England Pineapple pattern, attributed to the Boston and Sandwich Glass Works; made in the 1860's.
[*The Corning Museum of Glass*]

c Spoonholder, ribbed bellflower pattern, made about mid-nineteenth century.
[*The Corning Museum of Glass*]

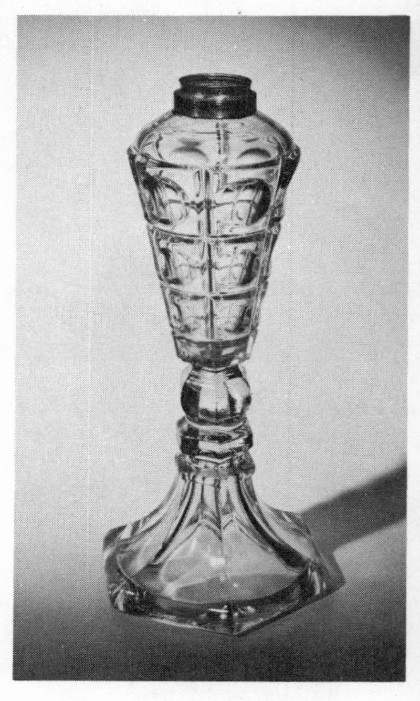

Plate 73
Pressed glass vase and lamp attributed to the Boston and Sandwich Glass Works, about 1850–1860. Here, the same mold has been used to make bases for both the lamp and the vase. [*The Corning Museum of Glass*]

a *b* *c*

Plate 74 ART GLASS

a Royal Flemish cracker jar made by the Mt. Washington Glass Company, New Bedford, Massachusetts, about 1890.

b Pomona vase. This type of glass was patented by Joseph Locke of the New England Glass Company in 1883.

c "Morgan" peachblow vase and holder made by the Hobbs-Brockunier Glass Works, Wheeling, West Virginia, about 1885. [*The Corning Museum of Glass*]

Plate 75
Plate cut with the Russian pattern by T. G. Hawkes & Co., Corning, New York, about 1900. [*The Corning Museum of Glass*]

sealing was necessary in order to protect the mercury coating from the effects of the atmosphere. Numerous other American glass companies also produced such wares, including the Union Glass Company of Somerville, Massachusetts, The Boston Silver Glass Company of Cambridge, Massachusetts, The Mt. Washington Glass Company of New Bedford, Massachusetts, The Brooklyn Flint Glass Company of Brooklyn, New York, and Dithridge & Company of Pittsburgh, Pennsylvania. It was primarily produced in this country between 1855 and 1885.

The earliest of the parti-colored glasses seems to be Amberina, patented in July 1883 by Joseph Locke, of the New England Glass Company. The gradual shading of this glass from amber to ruby is due to the presence of minute quantities of metallic gold. When just made, the entire glass has an amber color, but upon reheating, tiny metallic gold particles are formed in the glass and produce a ruby or fuchsia color. The same kind of glass was made by the Mt. Washington Glass Company, and termed variously Amberina, Rose Amberina, and Rose Amber. The production of this type of glass by the latter company resulted in a lawsuit brought by the New England Company, which was settled amicably, when the Mt. Washington Company agreed to restrict itself to the use of the term Rose Amber, instead of Amberina.

Amberina met with such commercial success that Frederick Shirley, Superintendent of the Mt. Washington Glass Works, developed and patented on December 15, 1885, an opaque glass shading from a light lemon-yellow color at the base to a plush peachy-rose near the top, which he termed Burmese. This ware proved to be extremely popular and was produced in a wide variety of forms, some of which were decorated with enameling. Shirley was an Englishman, and apparently an astute businessman. He sent a gift of decorated Burmese glass to Queen Victoria and Princess Beatrice, as well as to President Cleveland's wife, and named a pattern of the decorated Burmese for his former sovereign. As a result of the former gift, Burmese was also patented in England and produced there by Thomas Webb and Son, under license to the Mt. Washington Glass Company.

Another form of shaded ware which was popular in this period, and which is much sought after by collectors today, is Peach Blow glass. Two forms of this glass shading from an opaque white to a pink, or bluish pink, were produced by the New England Glass

Company and the Mt. Washington Glass Company in Massachusetts, and another form cased on the inside with an entirely creamy white glass, shading on the exterior from yellow at the base to a deep orangy-red color at the top was made by the Hobbs-Brockunier of Wheeling, West Virginia. Of these several Peach Blows, the one produced by the Hobbs-Brockunier Works was commercially the most successful; apparently only limited quantities of the Mt. Washington Peach Blow were made. It should be noted that a controversy over this shaded type of glass developed between the New England Glass Company and the Mt. Washington Glass Company, and the former agreed to call its wares Wild Rose, leaving the term Peach Blow to the Mt. Washington Glass Company, which had obtained a patent for this glass. "Satin" glass was another popular product of this era. It was usually made of at least two or more layers of different colored glasses, sometimes with air traps of diamond and herringbone patterns between the layers of glass, which is now frequently termed Mother-of-Pearl satin glass. Bowls, vases, and other objects of this type of glass, as well as the other art glasses already mentioned, were frequently made to be contained in silver-plated stands, which were in great vogue during the late Victorian period. Although only a few companies, such as the Mt. Washington Works and the Phoenix Glass Company of Pittsburgh, are definitely known to have produced art glass, it was undoubtedly also made in numerous other factories producing fine tablewares at this time.

Of all of the factories in America operating at this time, the Mt. Washington Glass Company, which frequently advertised itself as "headquarters for art glass in America," was probably the most prolific producer of art glasses. William Libbey, who left this company in 1872 to become agent for the New England Glass Company, had established a large decorating department in the former factory in 1871. As a result, numerous enameled and gilded glasses were among this company's production. Among them, dating from the late 1880's, were Albertine glass, a name later changed to Crown Milano, apparently to promote wider sales, and Royal Flemish, a transparent glass that was decorated in a fashion akin to stained-glass windows.

Opalescent glasses of various colors often with raised, molded designs such as "hobnail" and "Spanish lace" were also popular

Plate 76
Left to right: Aurene vase with floral trailings. Steuben Glass Works, Corning, New York, 1904–1915. Favrile, Jack-in-the-Pulpit vase. Glass Factory of Louis Comfort Tiffany, Corona, New York, 1900–1915. Height 13 inches. Favrile bowl, Glass Factory of Louis Comfort Tiffany, Corona, New York, 1900–1920. [*The Corning Museum of Glass*]

Plate 77 SEA CENTERPIECE
A crystal centerpiece suggesting the sea. Around the base are four wavelike scrolls. A fish leaps from the top of the cover, aided in its flight by thrusting waves. Height 11½ inches. [*Steuben Glass*]

during this 1870 to 1900 period. These wares were produced in numerous factories in both Europe and America.

CUT GLASS—THE BRILLIANT PERIOD

During the last ten or fifteen years of the nineteenth century and until about the beginning of World War I, fine cut glass enjoyed a revival and a great popularity, though its cost of production made it an item for the "carriage trade." Because the overall, multi-faceted patterns executed on fine quality lead glass resulted in brilliant and sparking effects, this period in the history of cut glass is referred to as the "brilliant period." An excellent example of this type of cutting is illustrated by the plate cut with the Russian pattern, in use between 1882 and 1900, shown in Plate 75. A complete set of stemware in this design, but bearing the Federal coat of arms, was ordered for a White House service in 1886 for Grover Cleveland. Additions to this service were made during the terms of Benjamin Harrison and Theodore Roosevelt.

ART NOUVEAU

Simultaneously with the development of the brilliant period of cut glass occurs the *art nouveau* style. This self-consciously developed "new art" was well expressed in the medium of glass by numerous proponents of this style in both America and Europe. The foremost of these in this country was Louis Comfort Tiffany, who had become well known in the 1880's for his stained-glass windows, and who turned to making other glass objects in the art nouveau style about 1892. This style was based primarily upon a return to more simplified, naturalistic motifs frequently expressed in objects taking the form of flowers, or being decorated by foliate or floral designs. Tiffany was also influenced by the iridescence on ancient glasses which had been caused by moisture in the soil in which they had been buried for so many years. He successfully combined all of these elements in a great variety of ways in the glasses he designed and which were made under his guidance. Tiffany termed not only his glass productions but some of his metal work and ceramics as well, *favrile*, a word he coined based upon the Latin word *faber*, "to make" (*Plate 76*).

Frederick Carder, an Englishman who came to this country in

1903 and founded Steuben Glass Works, was another prominent artist-craftsman who produced works in the art nouveau style in the early twentieth century. *Aurene* was a term applied by Carder to his iridescent glasses of this period, some of which were also further decorated with applied designs such as foliate motifs, chains and the like. The most elaborate and detailed of these glasses were produced between 1904 and 1918, when Steuben Glass Works became a division of Corning Glass Works. After this, Steuben, of which Mr. Carder became the art director, continued to produce simpler varieties, along with a wide variety of colored glasswares. In 1933 the company was reorganized and the production of colored glass discontinued.

Other American glass companies and designers of art nouveau glasses include the Union Glass Works, which termed its glasswares of this type "Kew-Blas," an anagram of W. S. Blake, then superintendent of the works. Martin Bach, Sr., a former employee of Tiffany's, set up his own glasshouse in Brooklyn, and produced similar glass which he termed *Quezal*, after the quetzal bird, whose plumage was brilliant, multi-colored, and iridescent. The Durand Glass Company, of Vineland, New Jersey, the Handel Company of Meriden, Connecticut, and the Honesdale Glass Decorating Company of Honesdale, Pennsylvania, as well as the Imperial Company of Bellaire, Ohio, produced decorative glasses in the art nouveau style, which gradually declined in the late 1920's and expired in the early 1930's.

As is usually the case, when one style expires another takes its place. In the 1930's, the pendulum swung back to colorless glass, sometimes sparsely engraved. From the 1920's to the early 1940's the Pairpoint Corporation of New Bedford and the Libbey Glass Company of Toledo were noteworthy for such production, but the most outstanding glass of this type was that produced by Steuben Glass, which since 1933 has concentrated on the production of fine quality wares of brilliant, colorless metal. Utmost attention has been paid by this firm to the design of forms noted for their restraint and classical feeling, while at the same time they have reached out and explored new means of working with this fine material. Today the glass and designs of this company stand as the epitome of purity and excellence (*Plate 77*).

Within the last few years there has been a growing interest on the part of individual craftsmen to produce art objects of glass in the studio, just as the potter produces ceramics on an individual basis. With the development of new refractory materials and temperature controls, and the widespread availability of natural gas and electricity, the exploration of glass as a medium for artistic expression is now coming within reach of the individual artist-craftsman. In the near future it is quite likely that we shall see the results of their creativity.

Chapter Thirteen

CONCLUSION

HOW should one start making a collection? The answer will depend on the kind of person you are, for any collection you make, whether it be modest or costly, must be a reflection of your personality. A collection is the result of selection, and selection is governed by personal taste and predilection.

If your aim is to gather pieces that are decorative, you will select for design and good craftsmanship and for qualities of aesthetic appeal. All old glass, even when it is valuable, is not necessarily lovely in itself, and if beauty is your object you will reject the merely curious or scarce. Indeed, from this point of view a machine-made article that has the merit of good design may give far more pleasure than a hand-wrought one in which the craftsmanship is second-rate. Then again, you might select a beautiful piece even if it has been broken and repaired or has a bit missing. Such pieces can usually be displayed in a way that hides the damaged part and, in that case, a crack or chip hardly detracts from the pleasure it can give you.

On the other hand, if you collect as an investment your selection will be governed by far different considerations. You will be likely to reject any piece that is cracked or even slightly chipped even if these defects are hardly noticeable, for imperfect pieces have only a fraction of the marketable value of those that are whole and undamaged.

If investment is your aim, you must be able to forecast future trends. You know what is the fashionable taste today, but can you tell what will be most admired fifty years hence? One can say with certainty that good eighteenth-century glass, for instance, will increase in value with the years, but what of the work of the generation previous to ours? The work of the immediate past is only old enough to be out of fashion, in many instances, but too young to be antique, in the true sense of the word. Nevertheless, much of this glass is "collectable," and it is in such marginal cases that one will find a fascinating pursuit in forecasting the future, and one's success as a collector will depend on astuteness, imagination, and a good slice of luck.

Others may collect from an interest in history, and, in this, glass will be a perpetual reminder of the customs of past generations in which may be discerned an unfolding social pattern. This aspect, indeed, is never absent whatever the motives of making a collection may be, and those who can cherish the subleties of the craftsmanship of the past are doing a service valuable not only to themselves but to future generations.

With glass, the beginner has difficulties not present in other subjects. China, for instance, has the guide of trademarks and the qualities of glaze or color to enable one to make a classification in periods of time, but glass has no distinguishing features of this kind. The making of fakes, therefore, holds a temptation all glassmakers are not able to resist. Usually, however, the fake does not impose on those who have had experience in handling genuine work.

The knowledge to judge these things can be had only by repeated experience. When one has handled old glass for a time one gets to know its qualities, and, in time, a kind of sixth sense is acquired that helps to protect one from the deception of fakes. How is the necessary experience gained if one starts with nothing? By calling on dealers and making friends of other collectors and by frequent visits to museums.

Museum collections, indeed, will be found of great value, not only in giving one a knowledge of craftsmanship and styles but in forming good taste. Familiarity with the best in the past gives one a standard by which all workmanship may be measured. Unconsciously the taste is formed by these higher standards, and meretricious work is robbed of its appeal. When only the really good can give satisfaction, one is on the way to acquire good taste and, with good taste, sound judgment. In this, museums will be found of the greatest assistance and, while one should visit the museum in one's locality frequently, it is a good policy never to miss an opportunity of visiting other museums when traveling away from home.

Glass is a very wide subject, and the man who starts a collection will find that it leads to the study not only of matters directly connected with the art, but with history and art generally. Thus an interest in glass extends one's knowledge over a wide field, quickens one's interest, and gives a zest for living that will have beneficial results not limited to the relaxation of collecting but extending into every activity of life.

In this volume I do not pretend to do more than introduce the subject, but, even so, I hope I have shown something of its range and scope, and, at the least, that I have set the traveler's feet on the right path. At any rate, these desultory chats have brought pleasure to one person, and it is with regret that I now lay aside my completed task to bid you farewell and wish you happy hunting.

Appendix

WHERE THE BEST PUBLIC COLLECTIONS OF GLASS ARE TO BE FOUND

THE undernoted comprise a selected list of British and American museums holding collections of glass. This list is by no means complete and leaves out of account small collections that are not wide in scope. The principal museums for glass are marked by an asterisk.

BRITISH MUSEUMS

BARNARD CASTLE: Bowes Museum. Some good glass.

BATH: Victoria Art Gallery. Flint and other glass.

BEDFORD: Higgins Museum. Fine collection of European and English glass.

BIRMINGHAM: Birmingham Art Gallery. Lead crystal and Venetian glass.

BRISTOL: Bristol Museum and Art Gallery. Good collection of eighteenth- and nineteenth-century colored glass. Lead crystal.

BUXTON: Buxton Museum. Lead crystal. English colored glass.

CAMBRIDGE: Fitzwilliam Museum and University Museum of Archaeology and Ethnology.*

CANTERBURY: Canterbury Museum. English medieval glass.

CARDIFF: National Museum of Wales. Eighteenth-century bottles and silver-mounted lead crystal.

Dublin: The National Museum of Antiquities.*

Edinburgh: Royal Scottish Museum* and National Museum of Antiquities.*

Exeter: Royal Albert Memorial Museum. Good collection of lead crystal.

Farnham, Dorset: Pitt-Rivers Museum. Good collection of ancient glass.

Glasgow: Kelvingrove Art Gallery. Good collection of Syrian glass. Venetian, Spanish, and German glass. Good loan collection of lead crystal.

Ipswich: Christchurch Mansion. Medieval fragments. Good collection of flint glass.

Leeds: City Museum. Murrines and ancient glass.

Liverpool: Liverpool Public Museums. Ancient glass. Good examples of post-Renaissance European glass. German glass. Bristol.

London: British Museum.* Victoria and Albert Museum.*
Guildhall Museum. Good collection of ancient glass from London sites. English lead crystal. Good collection of bottles and phials.
London Museum. The Garton collection of lead crystal. Good collection of bottles.
Science Museum. Reconstructions of ancient glasshouses in scale models. Process exhibits.

Manchester: City Art Gallery. Good collection of lead crystal. Examples of South Lancashire glass of eighteenth century.
University Museum. Syrian and Egyptian glass. Good examples of Alexandrian cut crystal. The Hawara vase is there, the best of its kind in Britain.

Newcastle-upon-Tyne: Black Gate Museum. Seine-Rhine fragments.
Laing Art Gallery. Good collection. Newcastle, Gateshead, and North Country glass of eighteenth and nineteenth centuries.

Oldham: Municipal Art Gallery. Part of F. Buckley collection, mostly North Country.

Oxford: Ashmolean Museum.*

SHEFFIELD: Weston Park Museum. Syrian glass. German glass and lead crystal of Yorkshire manufacture.
Society of Glass Technology. Good collection of recent glass.
Shipley Technical School Museum. Technical glass exhibits.

TRURO: Cornwall County Museum. Lead crystal and other glass.

YORK: Yorkshire Philosophical Society Museum. Seine-Rhine glass. Good collection of lead crystal and bottles.

AMERICAN MUSEUMS

BALTIMORE, MD.: Baltimore Museum of Art, Maryland Historical Society, Walters Gallery.

BOSTON, MASS.: Museum of Fine Arts.

BROOKLYN, N.Y.: Brooklyn Museum.*

CHICAGO, ILL.: Art Institute of Chicago.

CLEVELAND, OHIO: Cleveland Museum of Art.

CORNING, N.Y.: The Corning Museum of Glass.*

DEARBORN, MICH.: The Henry Ford Museum and Greenfield Village.*

MANCHESTER, N.H.: The Currier Gallery of Art.

NEW YORK, N.Y.: The Metropolitan Museum of Art.*

PHILADELPHIA, PA.: Philadelphia Museum of Art.*

SANDWICH, MASS.: The Sandwich Historical Society.*

ST. LOUIS, MO.: City Art Museum of St. Louis.

STURBRIDGE, MASS.: Old Sturbridge Village.*

TOLEDO, OHIO: The Toledo Museum of Art.*

Selected Bibliography

ENGLISH GLASS

BATE, PERCY. *English Tableglass.* New York: Charles Scribner's Sons, 1905.

BLES, JOSEPH. *Rare English Glasses of Seventeenth and Eighteenth Centuries.* Boston: Houghton Mifflin Company, 1925.

BUCKLEY, FRANCES. *History of Old English Glass.* New York: Dingwell-Rock Ltd., 1925.

BUCKLEY, WILFRED. *European Glass.* Boston: Houghton Mifflin Company, 1927.

———. *Diamond Engraved Glasses of the Sixteenth Century.* London: Ernest Benn Ltd., 1929.

———. *The Art of Glass.* New York: Oxford University Press, 1939.

DILLON, EDWARD. *Glass.* New York: G. P. Putnam's Sons, 1907.

ELVILLE, E. M. *English Tableglass.* New York: Charles Scribner's Sons, 1951.

FLEMING, JOHN ARNOLD. *Scottish and Jacobite Glass.* Glasgow: Jackson Son & Company, 1938.

HARTSHORNE, ALBERT. *Old English Glasses.* London and New York: E. Arnold, 1897.

HAYNES, E. BARRINGTON. *Glass Through the Ages.* Harmondsworth: Penguin Books [1948].

HONEY, WILLIAM BOWYER. *Glass: A Handbook and Guide to the Victoria and Albert Museum Collection.* London: The Victoria and Albert Museum, 1946.

HORRIDGE, W. "The Rose and Emblems on Jacobite Drinking Glasses," *Transactions of the Circle of Glass Collectors,* No. 56.

JANNEAU, GUILLAUME. *Modern Glass.* London: Studio Publications, 1936.

MARSON, PERCIVAL. *Glass.* London: Sir Isaac Pitman and Sons, 1918.

PELLATT, APSLEY. *Glass Manufactures.* London: B. J. Holdsworth, 1821.

———. *Curiosities of Glassmaking.* London: 1849.

PERCIVAL, MACIVER. *The Glass Collector.* New York: Dodd, Mead and Company, 1919.

POWELL, H. J. *Glassmaking in England.* New York and London: Macmillan Company, 1923.

THORPE, WILLIAM ARNOLD. *English Glass.* London: A. & C. Black Ltd., 1949.

WESTROPP, M. S. D. *Irish Glass.* Philadelphia: J. B. Lippincott Company, 1920.

AMERICAN GLASS

BELKNAP, E. MCCAMLY. *Milk Glass.* New York: Crown Publishers, Inc., 1949.

DANIEL, DOROTHY. *Cut and Engraved Glass, 1771–1905.* New York: M. Barrows and Company, 1950 (bibliography: pp. 420–424).

HUNTER, FREDERICK WILLIAM. *Stiegel Glass.* Boston: Houghton Mifflin Co., 1914.

INNES, LOWELL. *Early Glass of the Pittsburgh District, 1797–1890.* Pittsburgh: Exhibition at Carnegie Museum, 1949.

JARVES, DEMING. *Reminiscences of Glass-making.* Boston: Eastburn's Press, 1854.

KAMM, MINNIE WATSON. *Pitcher Books,* Numbers 1–8. Published by the author, 365 Lakeshore Road, Grosse Point Farms, Michigan.

LEE, RUTH WEBB. *Early American Pressed Glass.* Northboro, Mass.: published by the author, 1931.

———. *Handbook of Early American Pressed Glass Patterns,* Framingham Centre, Mass.: published by the author, 1936.

———. *Nineteenth Century Art Glass.* New York: M. Barrows and Co., Inc., 1952.

———. *Sandwich Glass,* Framingham Centre, Mass.: published by the author, 1939.

LEE, RUTH WEBB, and ROSE, JAMES H., *American Glass Cup Plates,* Northboro, Mass.: published by the authors, 1948.

MCKEARIN, GEORGE S., and HELEN. *American Glass.* New York: Crown Publications, 1948 (bibliography: pp. 615–617).

———. *Two Hundred Years of American Blown Glass.* New York: Crown Publications, 1950.

MCKEARIN, HELEN. *American Historical Flasks.* Corning, N.Y.: Corning Museum of Glass, 1953.

METZ, ALICE HULETT. *Early American Pattern Glass.* Westfield, N.Y.: Guide Publishing Co., 1958.

REVI, ALBERT CHRISTIAN. *American Pressed Glass and Figure Bottles.* New York: Thos. Nelson & Sons, 1964 (bibliography: p. 413).

———. *Nineteenth Century Glass: Its Genesis and Development.* New York: Thos. Nelson & Sons, 1959.

ROSE, JAMES H. *The Story of American Pressed Glass of the Lacy Period, 1825–1850.* Corning, N.Y.: Corning Museum of Glass, 1954.

THOMPSON, JAMES H. *Bitters Bottles.* Watkins Glen, N.Y.: Century House, 1946.

VAN RENSSELAER, STEPHEN. *American Bottles and Flasks.* Peterborough, N.H.: Transcript Printing Company, 1926 (revised, 2 vols.).

WATKINS, LURA WOODSIDE. *Cambridge Glass, 1818 to 1888.* Boston: Marshall Jones Co. [1930].

———. *American Glass and Glassmaking.* New York: Chanticleer Press, 1950.

WATSON, RICHARD. *Bitters Bottles.* New York, Thomas Nelson & Sons, 1965.

Index

Dover Books on Art

Dover Books on Art

THE FOUR BOOKS OF ARCHITECTURE, Andrea Palladio. A compendium of the art of Andrea Palladio, one of the most celebrated architects of the Renaissance, including 250 magnificently-engraved plates showing edifices either of Palladio's design or reconstructed (in these drawings) by him from classical ruins and contemporary accounts. 257 plates. xxiv + 119pp. 9½ x 12¾. T1308 Clothbound $10.00

150 MASTERPIECES OF DRAWING, A. Toney. Selected by a gifted artist and teacher, these are some of the finest drawings produced by Western artists from the early 15th to the end of the 18th centuries. Excellent reproductions of drawings by Rembrandt, Bruegel, Raphael, Watteau, and other familiar masters, as well as works by lesser known but brilliant artists. 150 plates. xviii + 150pp. 5⅜ x 11¼. T1032 Paperbound $2.00

MORE DRAWINGS BY HEINRICH KLEY. Another collection of the graphic, vivid sketches of Heinrich Kley, one of the most diabolically talented cartoonists of our century. The sketches take in every aspect of human life: nothing is too sacred for him to ridicule, no one too eminent for him to satirize. 158 drawings you will not easily forget. iv + 104pp. 7⅜ x 10¾. T41 Paperbound $1.85

THE TRIUMPH OF MAXIMILIAN I, 137 Woodcuts by Hans Burgkmair and Others. This is one of the world's great art monuments, a series of magnificent woodcuts executed by the most important artists in the German realms as part of an elaborate plan by Maximilian I, ruler of the Holy Roman Empire, to commemorate his own name, dynasty, and achievements. 137 plates. New translation of descriptive text, notes, and bibliography prepared by Stanley Appelbaum. Special section of 10pp. containing a reduced version of the entire Triumph. x + 169pp. 11⅛ x 9¼. T1207 Paperbound $3.00

LOST EXAMPLES OF COLONIAL ARCHITECTURE, J. M. Howells. This book offers a unique guided tour through America's architectural past, all of which is either no longer in existence or so changed that its original beauty has been destroyed. More than 275 clear photos of old churches, dwelling houses, public buildings, business structures, etc. 245 plates, containing 281 photos and 9 drawings, floorplans, etc. New Index. xvii + 248pp. 7⅞ x 10¾. T1143 Paperbound $2.75

200 DECORATIVE TITLE-PAGES, edited by A. Nesbitt. Fascinating and informative from a historical point of view, this beautiful collection of decorated titles will be a great inspiration to students of design, commercial artists, advertising designers, etc. A complete survey of the genre from the first known decorated title to work in the first decades of this century. Bibliography and sources of the plates. 222pp. 8⅜ x 11¼.
T1264 Paperbound $2.75

ON THE LAWS OF JAPANESE PAINTING, H. P. Bowie. This classic work on the philosophy and technique of Japanese art is based on the author's first-hand experiences studying art in Japan. Every aspect of Japanese painting is described: the use of the brush and other materials; laws governing conception and execution; subjects for Japanese paintings, etc. The best possible substitute for a series of lessons from a great Oriental master. Index. xv + 117pp. + 66 plates. 6⅛ x 9¼.
T30 Paperbound $2.25

PAINTING IN THE FAR EAST, L. Binyon. A study of over 1500 years of Oriental art by one of the world's outstanding authorities. The author chooses the most important masters in each period—Wu Tao-tzu, Toba Sojo, Kanaoka, Li Lung-mien, Masanobu, Okio, etc.—and examines the works, schools, and influence of each within their cultural context. 42 photographs. Sources of original works and selected bibliography. Notes including list of principal painters by periods. xx + 297pp. 6⅛ x 9¼.
T520 Paperbound $2.50

THE ALPHABET AND ELEMENTS OF LETTERING, F. W. Goudy. A beautifully illustrated volume on the aesthetics of letters and type faces and their history and development. Each plate consists of 15 forms of a single letter with the last plate devoted to the ampersand and the numerals. "A sound guide for all persons engaged in printing or drawing," Saturday Review. 27 full-page plates. 48 additional figures. xii + 131pp. 7⅞ x 10¾.
T792 Paperbound $2.25

PAINTING IN ISLAM, Sir Thomas W. Arnold. This scholarly study puts Islamic painting in its social and religious context and examines its relation to Islamic civilization in general. 65 full-page plates illustrate the text and give outstanding examples of Islamic art. 4 appendices. Index of mss. referred to. General Index. xxiv + 159pp. 6⅝ x 9¼. T1310 Paperbound $2.50

PRINCIPLES OF ART HISTORY, H. Wölfflin. This remarkably instructive work demonstrates the tremendous change in artistic conception from the 14th to the 18th centuries, by analyzing 164 works by Botticelli, Dürer, Hobbema, Holbein, Hals, Titian, Rembrandt, Vermeer, etc., and pointing out exactly what is meant by "baroque," "classic," "primitive," "picturesque," and other basic terms of art history and criticism. "A remarkable lesson in the art of seeing," SAT. REV. OF LITERATURE. Translated from the 7th German edition. 150 illus. 254pp. 6⅛ x 9¼. T276 Paperbound $2.00

FOUNDATIONS OF MODERN ART, A. Ozenfant. Stimulating discussion of human creativity from paleolithic cave painting to modern painting, architecture, decorative arts. Fully illustrated with works of Gris, Lipchitz, Léger, Picasso, primitive, modern artifacts, architecture, industrial art, much more. 226 illustrations. 368pp. 6⅛ x 9¼. T215 Paperbound $2.50

METALWORK AND ENAMELLING, H. Maryon. Probably the best book ever written on the subject. Tells everything necessary for the home manufacture of jewelry, rings, ear pendants, bowls, etc. Covers materials, tools, soldering, filigree, setting stones, raising patterns, repoussé work, damascening, niello, cloisonné, polishing, assaying, casting, and dozens of other techniques. The best substitute for apprenticeship to a master metalworker. 363 photos and figures. 374pp. 5½ x 8½. T183 Clothbound $8.50

SHAKER FURNITURE, E. D. and *F. Andrews.* The most illuminating study of Shaker furniture ever written. Covers chronology, craftsmanship, houses, shops, etc. Includes over 200 photographs of chairs, tables, clocks, beds, benches, etc. "Mr. & Mrs. Andrews know all there is to know about Shaker furniture," Mark Van Doren, NATION. 48 full-page plates. 192pp. 7⅞ x 10¾. T679 Paperbound $2.25

ANIMAL DRAWING: ANATOMY AND ACTION FOR ARTISTS, C. R. Knight. 158 studies, with full accompanying text, of such animals as the gorilla, bear, bison, dromedary, camel, vulture, pelican, iguana, shark, etc., by one of the greatest modern masters of animal drawing. Innumerable tips on how to get life expression into your work. "An excellent reference work," SAN FRANCISCO CHRONICLE. 158 illustrations. 156pp. 10½ x 8½. T426 Paperbound $2.75

Dover Books on Art

AFRICAN SCULPTURE, Ladislas Segy. 163 full-page plates illustrating masks, fertility figures, ceremonial objects, etc., of 50 West and Central African tribes—95% never before illustrated. 34-page introduction to African sculpture. "Mr. Segy is one of its top authorities," NEW YORKER. 164 full-page photographic plates. Introduction. Bibliography. 244pp. $6\frac{1}{8}$ x $9\frac{1}{4}$.
T396 Paperbound $2.25

CALLIGRAPHY, J. G. Schwandner. First reprinting in 200 years of this legendary book of beautiful handwriting. Over 300 ornamental initials, 12 complete calligraphic alphabets, over 150 ornate frames and panels, 75 calligraphic pictures of cherubs, stags, lions, etc., thousands of flourishes, scrolls, etc., by the greatest 18th-century masters. All material can be copied or adapted without permission. Historical introduction. 158 full-page plates. 368pp. 9 x 13. T475 Clothbound $10.00

A DIDEROT PICTORIAL ENCYCLOPEDIA OF TRADES AND INDUSTRY. Manufacturing and the Technical Arts in Plates Selected from "L'Encyclopédie ou Dictionnaire Raisonné des Sciences, des Arts, et des Métiers," of Denis Diderot, edited with text by C. Gillispie. Over 2000 illustrations on 485 full-page plates. Magnificent 18th-century engravings of men, women, and children working at such trades as milling flour, cheesemaking, charcoal burning, mining, silverplating, shoeing horses, making fine glass, printing, hundreds more, showing details of machinery, different steps in sequence, etc. A remarkable art work, but also the largest collection of working figures in print, copyright-free, for art directors, designers, etc. Two vols. 920pp. 9 x 12. Heavy library cloth. T421 Two volume set $22.50

SILK SCREEN TECHNIQUES, J. Biegeleisen, M. Cohn. A practical step-by-step home course in one of the most versatile, least expensive graphic arts processes. How to build an inexpensive silk screen, prepare stencils, print, achieve special textures, use color, etc. Every step explained, diagrammed. 149 illustrations, 201pp. $6\frac{1}{8}$ x $9\frac{1}{4}$. T433 Paperbound $2.00

STICKS AND STONES, Lewis Mumford. An examination of forces influencing American architecture: the medieval tradition in early New England, the classical influence in Jefferson's time, the Brown Decades, the imperial facade, the machine age, etc. "A truly remarkable book," SAT. REV. OF LITERATURE. 2nd revised edition. 21 illus. xvii + 240pp. $5\frac{3}{8}$ x 8.
T202 Paperbound $2.00

Dover Books on Art

ART ANATOMY, Dr. William Rimmer. One of the few books on art anatomy that are themselves works of art, this is a faithful reproduction (rearranged for handy use) of the extremely rare masterpiece of the famous 19th century anatomist, sculptor, and art teacher. Beautiful, clear line drawings show every part of the body—bony structure, muscles, features, etc. Unusual are the sections on falling bodies, foreshortenings, muscles in tension, grotesque personalities, and Rimmer's remarkable interpretation of emotions and personalities as expressed by facial features. It will supplement every other book on art anatomy you are likely to have. Reproduced clearer than the lithographic original (which sells for $500 on up on the rare book market.) Over 1,200 illustrations. xiii + 153pp. $7\frac{3}{4}$ x $10\frac{3}{4}$.
T908 Paperbound $2.25

THE CRAFTSMAN'S HANDBOOK, Cennino Cennini. The finest English translation of IL LIBRO DELL' ARTE, the 15th century introduction to art technique that is both a mirror of Quatrocento life and a source of many useful but nearly forgotten facets of the painter's art. 4 illustrations. xxvii + 142pp. D. V. Thompson, translator. $5\frac{3}{8}$ x 8. T54 Paperbound $1.75

THE BROWN DECADES, Lewis Mumford. A picture of the "buried renaissance" of the post-Civil War period, and the founding of modern architecture (Sullivan, Richardson, Root, Roebling), landscape development (Marsh, Olmstead, Eliot), and the graphic arts (Homer, Eakins, Ryder). 2nd revised, enlarged edition. Bibliography. 12 illustrations. xiv + 266 pp. $5\frac{3}{8}$ x 8.
T200 Paperbound $1.75

THE HUMAN FIGURE, J. H. Vanderpoel. Not just a picture book, but a complete course by a famous figure artist. Extensive text, illustrated by 430 pencil and charcoal drawings of both male and female anatomy. 2nd enlarged edition. Foreword. 430 illus. 143pp. $6\frac{1}{8}$ x $9\frac{1}{4}$. T432 Paperbound $1.45

PINE FURNITURE OF EARLY NEW ENGLAND, R. H. Kettell. Over 400 illustrations, over 50 working drawings of early New England chairs, benches, beds, cupboards, mirrors, shelves, tables, other furniture esteemed for simple beauty and character. "Rich store of illustrations . . . emphasizes the individuality and varied design," ANTIQUES. 413 illustrations, 55 working drawings. 475pp. 8 x $10\frac{3}{4}$. T145 Clothbound $10.00

Dover Books on Art

MASTERPIECES OF FURNITURE, Verna Cook Salomonsky. Photographs and measured drawings of some of the finest examples of Colonial American, 17th century English, Windsor, Sheraton, Hepplewhite, Chippendale, Louis XIV, Queen Anne, and various other furniture styles. The textual matter includes information on traditions, characteristics, background, etc. of various pieces. 101 plates. Bibliography. 224pp. $7\frac{7}{8}$ x $10\frac{3}{4}$.
T1381 Paperbound $2.00

PRIMITIVE ART, Franz Boas. In this exhaustive volume, a great American anthropologist analyzes all the fundamental traits of primitive art, covering the formal element in art, representative art, symbolism, style, literature, music, and the dance. Illustrations of Indian embroidery, paleolithic paintings, woven blankets, wing and tail designs, totem poles, cutlery, earthenware, baskets and many other primitive objects and motifs. Over 900 illustrations. 376pp. $5\frac{3}{8}$ x 8. T25 Paperbound $2.25

AN INTRODUCTION TO A HISTORY OF WOODCUT, A. M. Hind. Nearly all of this authoritative 2-volume set is devoted to the 15th century—the period during which the woodcut came of age as an important art form. It is the most complete compendium of information on this period, the artists who contributed to it, and their technical and artistic accomplishments. Profusely illustrated with cuts by 15th century masters, and later works for comparative purposes. 484 illustrations. 5 indexes. Total of xi + 838pp. $5\frac{3}{8}$ x $8\frac{1}{2}$. Two-volume set, T952-3 Paperbound $5.00

ART STUDENTS' ANATOMY, E. J. Farris. Teaching anatomy by using chiefly living objects for illustration, this study has enjoyed long popularity and success in art courses and home-study programs. All the basic elements of the human anatomy are illustrated in minute detail, diagrammed and pictured as they pass through common movements and actions. 158 drawings, photographs, and roentgenograms. Glossary of anatomical terms. x + 159pp. $5\frac{5}{8}$ x $8\frac{3}{8}$. T744 Paperbound $1.50

COLONIAL LIGHTING, A. H. Hayward. The only book to cover the fascinating story of lamps and other lighting devices in America. Beginning with rush light holders used by the early settlers, it ranges through the elaborate chandeliers of the Federal period, illustrating 647 lamps. Of great value to antique collectors, designers, and historians of arts and crafts. Revised and enlarged by James R. Marsh. xxxi + 198pp. $5\frac{5}{8}$ x $8\frac{1}{4}$.
T975 Paperbound $2.00

GREEK REVIVAL ARCHITECTURE IN AMERICA, T. Hamlin. A comprehensive study of the American Classical Revival its regional variations, reasons for its success and eventual decline. Profusely illustrated with photos, sketches, floor plans and sections, displaying the work of almost every important architect of the time. 2 appendices. 39 figures, 94 plates containing 221 photos, 62 architectural designs, drawings, etc. 324-item classified bibliography. Index. xi + 439pp. $5\frac{3}{8}$ x $8\frac{1}{2}$.
T1148 Paperbound $3.00

CREATIVE LITHOGRAPHY AND HOW TO DO IT, Grant Arnold. Written by a man who practiced and taught lithography for many years, this highly useful volume explains all the steps of the lithographic process from tracing the drawings on the stone to printing the lithograph, with helpful hints for solving special problems. Index. 16 reproductions of lithographs. 11 drawings. xv + 214pp. of text. $5\frac{3}{8}$ x $8\frac{1}{2}$.
T1208 Paperbound $1.65

TEACH YOURSELF ANTIQUE COLLECTING, E. Bradford. An excellent, brief guide to collecting British furniture, silver, pictures and prints, pewter, pottery and porcelain, Victoriana, enamels, clocks or other antiques. Much background information difficult to find elsewhere. 15pp. of illus. 215pp. 7 x $4\frac{1}{4}$.
Clothbound $2.00

THE STANDARD BOOK OF QUILT MAKING AND COLLECTING, M. Ickis. Even if you are a beginner, you will soon find yourself quilting like an expert, by following these clearly drawn patterns, photographs, and step-by-step instructions. Learn how to plan the quilt, to select the pattern to harmonize with the design and color of the room, to choose materials. Over 40 full-size patterns. Index. 483 illustrations. One color plate. xi + 276pp. $6\frac{3}{4}$ x $9\frac{1}{2}$. T582 Paperbound $2.00

THE ENJOYMENT AND USE OF COLOR, W. Sargent. Requiring no special technical know-how, this book tells you all about color and how it is created, perceived, and imitated in art. Covers many little-known facts about color values, intensities, effects of high and low illumination, complementary colors, and color harmonies. Simple do-it-yourself experiments and observations. 35 illustrations, including 6 full-page color plates. New color frontispiece. Index. x + 274 pp. $5\frac{3}{8}$ x 8.
T944 Paperbound $2.00

LANDSCAPE GARDENING IN JAPAN, Josiah Conder. A detailed picture of Japanese gardening techniques and ideas, the artistic principles incorporated in the Japanese garden, and the religious and ethical concepts at the heart of those principles. Preface. 92 illustrations, plus all 40 full-page plates from the Supplement. Index. xv + 299pp. 8⅜ x 11¼.
T1216 Paperbound $3.50

DESIGN AND FIGURE CARVING, E. J. Tangerman. "Anyone who can peel a potato can carve," states the author, and in this unusual book he shows you how, covering every stage in detail from very simple exercises working up to museum-quality pieces. Terrific aid for hobbyists, arts and crafts counselors, teachers, those who wish to make reproductions for the commercial market. Appendix: How to Enlarge a Design. Brief bibliography. Index. 1298 figures. x + 289pp. 5⅜ x 8½.
T1209 Paperbound $1.85

WILD FOWL DECOYS, Joel Barber. Antique dealers, collectors, craftsmen, hunters, readers of Americana, etc. will find this the only thorough and reliable guide on the market today to this unique folk art. It contains the history, cultural significance, regional design variations; unusual decoy lore; working plans for constructing decoys; and loads of illustrations. 140 full-page plates, 4 in color. 14 additional plates of drawings and plans by the author. xxvii + 156pp. 7⅞ x 10¾. T11 Paperbound $3.50

1800 WOODCUTS BY THOMAS BEWICK AND HIS SCHOOL. This is the largest collection of first-rate pictorial woodcuts in print—an indispensable part of the working library of every commercial artist, art director, production designer, packaging artist, craftsman, manufacturer, librarian, art collector, and artist. And best of all, when you buy your copy of Bewick, you buy the rights to reproduce individual illustrations—no permission needed, no acknowledgments, no clearance fees! Classified index. Bibliography and sources. xiv + 246pp. 9 x 12.
T766 Clothbound $10.00

THE SCRIPT LETTER, Tommy Thompson. Prepared by a noted authority, this is a thorough, straightforward course of instruction with advice on virtually every facet of the art of script lettering. Also a brief history of lettering with examples from early copy books and illustrations from present day advertising and packaging. Copiously illustrated. Bibliography. 128pp. 6½ x 9⅛. T1311 Paperbound $1.50

THE HISTORY AND TECHNIQUE OF LETTERING, A. Nesbitt. A thorough history of lettering from the ancient Egyptians to the present, and a 65-page course in lettering for artists. Every major development in lettering history is illustrated by a complete aphabet. Fully analyzes such masters as Caslon, Koch, Garamont, Jenson, and many more. 89 alphabets, 165 other specimens. 317pp. 7½ x 10½. T427 Paperbound $2.25

LETTERING AND ALPHABETS, J. A. Cavanagh. An unabridged reissue of "Lettering," containing the full discussion, analysis, illustration of 89 basic hand lettering styles based on Caslon, Bodoni, Gothic, many other types. Hundreds of technical hints on construction, strokes, pens, brushes, etc. 89 alphabets, 72 lettered specimens, which may be reproduced permission-free. 121pp. 9¾ x 8. T53 Paperbound $1.50

THE HUMAN FIGURE IN MOTION, Eadweard Muybridge. The largest collection in print of Muybridge's famous high-speed action photos. 4789 photographs in more than 500 action-strip-sequences (at shutter speeds up to 1/6000th of a second) illustrate men, women, children—mostly undraped—performing such actions as walking, running, getting up, lying down, carrying objects, throwing, etc. "An unparalleled dictionary of action for all artists," AMERICAN ARTIST. 390 full-page plates, with 4789 photographs. Heavy glossy stock, reinforced binding with headbands. 7⅞ x 10¾. T204 Clothbound $10.00

ANIMALS IN MOTION, Eadweard Muybridge. The largest collection of animal action photos in print. 34 different animals (horses, mules, oxen, goats, camels, pigs, cats, lions, gnus, deer, monkeys, eagles—and 22 others) in 132 characteristic actions. All 3919 photographs are taken in series at speeds up to 1/1600th of a second, offering artists, biologists, cartoonists a remarkable opportunity to see exactly how an ostrich's head bobs when running, how a lion puts his foot down, how an elephant's knee bends, how a bird flaps his wings, thousands of other hard-to-catch details. "A really marvellous series of plates," NATURE. 380 full-page plates. Heavy glossy stock, reinforced binding with headbands. 7⅞ x 10¾. T203 Clothbound $10.00

BASIC BOOKBINDING, A. W. Lewis. Enables both beginners and experts to rebind old books or bind paperbacks in hard covers. Treats materials, tools; gives step-by-step instruction in how to collate a book, sew it, back it, make boards, etc. 261 illus. Appendices. 155pp. 5⅜ x 8. T169 Paperbound $1.50

Dover Books on Art

THE BOOK OF SIGNS, R. Koch. 493 symbols—crosses, monograms, astrological, biological symbols, runes, etc.—from ancient manuscripts, cathedrals, coins, catacombs, pottery. May be reproduced permission-free. 493 illustrations by Fritz Kredel. 104pp. 6⅛ x 9¼. T162 Paperbound $1.25

A HANDBOOK OF EARLY ADVERTISING ART, C. P. Hornung. The largest collection of copyright-free early advertising art ever compiled. Vol. I: 2,000 illustrations of animals, old automobiles, buildings, allegorical figures, fire engines, Indians, ships, trains, more than 33 other categories! Vol. II: Over 4,000 typographical specimens; 600 Roman, Gothic, Barnum, Old English faces; 630 ornamental type faces; hundreds of scrolls, initials, flourishes, etc. "A remarkable collection," PRINTERS' INK.

Vol. I: Pictorial Volume. Over 2000 illustrations. 256pp. 9 x 12. T122 Clothbound $10.00

Vol. II: Typographical Volume. Over 4000 specimens. 319pp. 9 x 12. T123 Clothbound $10.00

Two volume set, Clothbound, only $18.50

THE AUTOBIOGRAPHY OF AN IDEA, Louis Sullivan. The architect whom Frank Lloyd Wright called "the master," records the development of the theories that revolutionized America's skyline. 34 full-page plates of Sullivan's finest work. New introduction by R. M. Line. xiv + 335pp. 5⅜ x 8. T281 Paperbound $2.25

THE MATERIALS AND TECHNIQUES OF MEDIEVAL PAINTING, D. V. Thompson. An invaluable study of carriers and grounds, binding media, pigments, metals used in painting, al fresco and al secco techniques, burnishing, etc. used by the medieval masters. Preface by Bernard Berenson. 239pp. 5⅜ x 8. T327 Paperbound $2.00

HANDBOOK OF ORNAMENT, F. S. Meyer. One of the largest collections of copyright-free traditional art: over 3300 line cuts of Greek, Roman, Medieval, Renaissance, Baroque, 18th and 19th century art motifs (tracery, geometric elements, flower and animal motifs, etc.) and decorated objects (chairs, thrones, weapons, vases, jewelry, armor, etc.). Full text. 300 plates. 3300 illustrations. 562pp. 5⅜ x 8. T302 Paperbound $2.75

HAWTHORNE ON PAINTING. Vivid re-creation, from students' notes, of instructions by Charles Hawthorne at Cape Cod School of Art. Essays, epigrammatic comments on color, form, seeing, techniques, etc. "Excellent," Time. 100pp. 5$\frac{3}{8}$ x 8.
T653 Paperbound $1.25

THE HANDBOOK OF PLANT AND FLORAL ORNAMENT, R. G. Hatton. 1200 line illustrations, from medieval, Renaissance herbals, of flowering or fruiting plants: garden flowers, wild flowers, medicinal plants, poisons, industrial plants, etc. A unique compilation that probably could not be matched in any library in the world. Formerly "The Craftsman's Plant-Book." Also full text on uses, history as ornament, etc. 548pp. 6$\frac{1}{8}$ x 9$\frac{1}{4}$.
T649 Paperbound $3.50

DECORATIVE ALPHABETS AND INITIALS, Alexander Nesbitt. 91 complete alphabets, over 3900 ornamental initials, from Middle Ages, Renaissance printing, baroque, rococo, and modern sources. Individual items copyright free, for use in commercial art, crafts, design, packaging, etc. 123 full-page plates. 3924 initials. 129pp. 7$\frac{3}{4}$ x 10$\frac{3}{4}$. T544 Paperbound $2.50

METHODS AND MATERIALS OF THE GREAT SCHOOLS AND MASTERS, Sir Charles Eastlake. (Formerly titled "Materials for a History of Oil Painting.") Vast, authentic reconstruction of secret techniques of the masters, recreated from ancient manuscripts, contemporary accounts, analysis of paintings, etc. Oils, fresco, tempera, varnishes, encaustics. Both Flemish and Italian schools, also British and French. One of great works for art historians, critics; inexhaustible mine of suggestions, information for practicing artists. Total of 1025pp. 5$\frac{3}{8}$ x 8.
Two volume set, T718-9 Paperbound $5.00

BYZANTINE ART AND ARCHAEOLOGY, O. M. Dalton. Still most thorough work in English on Byzantine art forms throughout ancient and medieval world. Analyzes hundreds of pieces, covers sculpture, painting, mosaic, jewelry, textiles, architecture, etc. Historical development; specific examples; iconology and ideas; symbolism. A treasure-trove of material about one of most important art traditions, will supplement and expand any other book in area. Bibliography of over 2500 items. 457 illustrations. 747pp. 6$\frac{1}{8}$ x 9$\frac{1}{4}$. T776 Clothbound $8.50

'OOT-HIGH LETTERS: A GUIDE TO LETTERING, M. Price. ,8 $15\frac{1}{2}$ x $22\frac{1}{2}''$ plates, give classic Roman alphabet, one foot ıigh per letter, plus 9 other 2″ high letter forms for each letter. 16 page syllabus. Ideal for lettering classes, home study. 28 plates n box. T239 $6.00

A HANDBOOK OF WEAVES, G. H. Oelsner. Most complete ›ook of weaves, fully explained, differentiated, illustrated. Plain veaves, irregular, double-stitched, filling satins; derivative, ›asket, rib weaves; steep, broken, herringbone, twills, lace, tricot, nany others. Translated, revised by S. S. Dale; supplement on ınalysis of weaves. Bible for all handweavers. 1875 illustrations. 410pp. $6\frac{1}{8}$ x $9\frac{1}{4}$. T209 Clothbound $6.00

'APANESE HOMES AND THEIR SURROUNDINGS, E. S. Morse. Classic describes, analyses, illustrates all aspects of tra-litional Japanese home, from plan and structure to appoint-nents, furniture, etc. Published in 1886, before Japanese archi-ecture was contaminated by Western, this is strikingly modern n beautiful, functional approach to living. Indispensable to every ırchitect, interior decorator, designer. 307 illustrations. Glossary. 410pp. $5\frac{5}{8}$ x $8\frac{3}{8}$. T746 Paperbound $2.50

THE DRAWINGS OF HEINRICH KLEY. Uncut publication of long-sought-after sketchbooks of satiric, ironic iconoclast. Re-narkable fantasy, weird symbolism, brilliant technique make Kley a shocking experience to layman, endless source of ideas, echniques for artist. 200 drawings, original size, captions trans-lated. Introduction. 136pp. 6 x 9. T24 Paperbound $2.00

COSTUMES OF THE ANCIENTS, Thomas Hope. Beautiful, clear, sharp line drawings of Greek and Roman figures in full costume, by noted artist and antiquary of early 19th century. Dress, armor, divinities, masks, etc. Invaluable sourcebook for costumers, designers, first-rate picture file for illustrators, com-mercial artists. Introductory text by Hope. 300 plates. 6 x 9. T21 Paperbound $2.00

VITRUVIUS: TEN BOOKS ON ARCHITECTURE. The most influential book in the history of architecture. 1st century A.D. Roman classic has influenced such men as Bramante, Palladio, Michelangelo, up to present. Classic principles of design, har-mony, etc. Fascinating reading. Definitive English translation by Professor H. Morgan, Harvard. 344pp. $5\frac{3}{8}$ x 8. T645 Paperbound $2.50

HANDBOOK OF DESIGNS AND DEVICES, C. P. Hornung. A remarkable working collection of 1836 basic designs and variations, all copyright-free. Variations of circle, line, cross, diamond, swastika, star, scroll, shield, many more. Notes on symbolism. "A necessity to every designer who would be original without having to labor heavily," ARTIST AND ADVERTISER. 204 plates. 240pp. 5⅜ x 8. T125 Paperbound $2.00

THE UNIVERSAL PENMAN, George Bickham. Exact reproduction of beautiful 18th-century book of handwriting. 22 complete alphabets in finest English roundhand, other scripts, over 2000 elaborate flourishes, 122 calligraphic illustrations, etc. Material is copyright-free. "An essential part of any art library, and a book of permanent value," AMERICAN ARTIST. 212 plates. 224pp. 9 x 13¾. T20 Clothbound $10.00

AN ATLAS OF ANATOMY FOR ARTISTS, F. Schider. This standard work contains 189 full-page plates, more than 647 illustrations of all aspects of the human skeleton, musculature, cutaway portions of the body, each part of the anatomy, hand forms, eyelids, breasts; location of muscles under the flesh, etc. 59 plates illustrate how Michelangelo, da Vinci, Goya, 15 others, drew human anatomy. New 3rd edition enlarged by 52 new illustrations by Cloquet, Barcsay. "The standard reference tool," AMERICAN LIBRARY ASSOCIATION. "Excellent," AMERICAN ARTIST. 189 plates, 647 illustrations. xxvi + 192pp. 7⅞ x 10⅝. T241 Clothbound $6.00

AN ATLAS OF ANIMAL ANATOMY FOR ARTISTS, W. Ellenberger, H. Baum, H. Dittrich. The largest, richest animal anatomy for artists in English. Form, musculature, tendons, bone structure, expression, detailed cross sections of head, other features, of the horse, lion, dog, cat, deer, seal, kangaroo, cow, bull, goat, monkey, hare, many other animals. "Highly recommended," DESIGN. Second, revised, enlarged edition with new plates from Cuvier, Stubbs, etc. 288 illustrations. 153pp. 11⅜ x 9. T82 Clothbound $6.00

VASARI ON TECHNIQUE, G. Vasari. Pupil of Michelangelo, outstanding biographer of Renaissance artists reveals technical methods of his day. Marble, bronze, fresco painting, mosaics, engraving, stained glass, rustic ware, etc. Only English translation, extensively annotated by G. Baldwin Brown. 18 plates. 342pp. 5⅜ x 8. T717 Paperbound $2.75